# The Battle of Marathon

**Books in the Battles Series:**

✦ BATTLES OF THE ANCIENT WORLD ✦

# The Battle of Marathon

**by Don Nardo**

Lucent Books, P.O. Box 289011, San Diego, CA 92198-9011

**Library of Congress Cataloging-in-Publication Data**

Nardo, Don, 1947–
    The battle of Marathon / by Don Nardo.
      p.   cm. — (Battles of the ancient world)
    Includes bibliographical references and index.
    ISBN 1-56006-412-9 (Lib. ed. : alk. paper)
    1. Marathon, Battle of, 490 B.C.—Juvenile literature. 2. Greece—
Civilization—To 146 B.C.—Juvenile literature. 3. Iran—History—
To 640 A.D.—Juvenile literature. [1. Marathon, Battle of, 490 B.C.
2. Greece—Civilization—To 146 B.C. 3. Iran—History—
To 640 A.D.]  I. Title. II Series.
DF225.4.N37   1996
938'.03—dc20                                    95-11710
                                              CIP
                                              AC

# Contents

# Foreword

Almost everyone would agree with William Tecumseh Sherman that war "is all hell." Yet the history of war, and battles in particular, is so fraught with the full spectrum of human emotion and action that it becomes a microcosm of the human experience. Soldiers' lives are condensed and crystallized in a single battle. As Francis Miller explains in his *Photographic History of the Civil War* when describing the war wounded, "It is sudden, the transition from marching bravely at morning on two sound legs, grasping your rifle in two sturdy arms, to lying at nightfall under a tree with a member forever gone."

Decisions made on the battlefield can mean the lives of thousands. A general's pique or indigestion can result in the difference between life and death. Some historians speculate, for example, that Napoleon's fateful defeat at Waterloo was due to the beginnings of stomach cancer. His stomach pain may have been the reason that the normally decisive general was sluggish and reluctant to move his troops. And what kept George McClellan from winning battles during the Civil War? Some scholars and contemporaries believe that it was simple cowardice and fear. Others argue that he felt a gut-wrenching unwillingness to engage in the war of attrition that was characteristic of that particular conflict.

Battle decisions can be magnificently brilliant and horribly costly. At the Battle of Thaspus in 47 B.C., for example, Julius Caesar, facing a numerically superior army, shrewdly ordered his troops onto a narrow strip of land bordering the sea. Just as he expected, his enemy thought he had accidentally trapped himself and divided their forces to surround his troops. By dividing their army, his enemy had given Caesar the strategic edge he needed to defeat them. Other battle orders result in disaster, as in the case of the Battle at Balaklava during the Crimean War in 1854. A British general gave the order to attack a force of withdrawing enemy Russians. But confusion in relaying the order resulted in the 670 men of the Light Brigade's charging in the wrong direction into certain death by heavy enemy cannon fire. Battles are the stuff of history on the grandest scale—their outcomes often determine whether nations are enslaved or liberated.

Moments in battles illustrate the best and worst of human character. In the feeling of terror and the us-versus-them attitude that accompanies war, the enemy can be dehumanized and treated with a contempt that is considered repellent in times of peace. At Wounded Knee, the distrust and anticipation of violence that grew between the Native Americans and American soldiers led to the senseless killing of ninety men, women, and children. And who can forget My Lai, where the deaths of old men, women, and children at the hands of American soldiers shocked an America already disillusioned with the Vietnam War. The murder of six million Jews will remain burned into the human conscience forever as the measure of man's inhumanity to man. These horrors cannot be forgotten. And yet, under the terrible conditions of battle, one can find acts of bravery, kindness, and altruism. During the Battle of Midway, the members of Torpedo Squadron 8, flying in hopelessly antiquated planes and without the benefit of air protection from fighters, tried bravely to fulfill their mission—to destroy the *Kido Butai,* the Japanese Carrier Striking Force. Without air support, the squadron was immediately set upon by Japanese fighters. Nevertheless, each bomber tried valiantly to hit his target. Each failed. Every man but one died in the effort. But by keeping the Japanese fighters busy, the squadron bought time and delayed further Japanese fighter attacks. In the aftermath of the Battle of Isandhlwana in South Africa in 1879, a force of thousands of Zulu warriors trapped a contingent of British troops in a small trading post. After repeated bloody attacks in which many died on both sides, the Zulus, their final victory certain, granted the remaining British their lives as a gesture of respect for their bravery. During World War I, American troops were so touched by the fate of French war orphans that they took up a collection to help them. During the Civil War, soldiers of the North and South would briefly forget that they were enemies and share smokes and coffee across battle lines during the endless nights. These acts seem all the more dramatic, more uplifting, because they indicate that people can continue to behave with humanity when faced with inhumanity.

Lucent Books' Battles Series highlights the vast range of the human character revealed in the ordeal of war. Dramatic narrative describes in exciting and accurate detail the commanders, soldiers, weapons, strategies, and maneuvers involved in each battle. Each volume includes a comprehensive historical context, explaining what brought the parties to war, the events leading to the battle, what factors made the battle important, and the effects it had on the larger war and later events.

The Battles Series also includes a chronology of important dates that gives students an overview, at a glance, of each battle. Sidebars create a broader context by adding enlightening details on leaders, institutions, customs, warships, weapons, and armor mentioned in the narration. Every volume contains numerous maps that allow readers to better visualize troop movements and strategies. In addition, numerous primary and secondary source quotations drawn from both past historical witnesses and modern historians are included. These quotations demonstrate to readers how and where historians derive information about past events. Finally, the volumes in the Battles Series provide a launching point for further reading and research. Each book contains a bibliography designed for student research, as well as a second bibliography that includes the works the author consulted while compiling the book.

Above all, the Battles Series helps illustrate the words of Herodotus, the fifth-century B.C. Greek historian now known as the "father of history." In the opening lines of his great chronicle of the Greek and Persian Wars, the world's first battle book, he set for himself this goal: "To preserve the memory of the past by putting on record the astonishing achievements both of our own and of other peoples; and more particularly, to show how they came into conflict."

# Chronology of Events

**B.C.**

**ca. 1200**
The Mycenaean Greeks sack the trading city of Troy, located in Asia Minor, initiating the first known clash between the European West and Asian East.

**ca. 1100**
Dorian invaders sweep down from southern Europe and overrun mainland Greece; many Mycenaeans flee to the coast of Asia Minor to found the Greek Ionian cities; Greece's dark age begins.

**ca. 1000–700**
City-states, or poleis, rise throughout mainland Greece, the islands of the Aegean Sea, and Ionia.

**ca. 750–675**
The warfare style featuring heavy infantry (or hoplites) and the rigid phalanx formation develops on the Greek mainland.

**621**
Responding to public pressure, an aristocrat named Draco formulates a set of laws for Athens, already the most populous and successful polis; the people soon find these laws too harsh.

**612**
In western Asia (now the Middle East), Nineveh, capital of the once powerful and warlike Assyrian Empire, falls to the combined forces of the Medes and the Babylonians.

**594**
Athenian leader Solon reorganizes the government, throws out most of Draco's laws, and introduces more just laws, taking important steps toward the establishment of democracy.

**585**
Cyaxares, king of the Medes, enters Asia Minor and attacks the Lydian kingdom, the immediate neighbor of the Ionian Greeks, bringing the powers of East and West into close proximity.

**561**
Popular Athenian general Pisistratus seizes power and becomes tyrant, or autocratic ruler, of Athens; however, his enlightened rule brings adherence to the laws and a burst of cultural activity rather than dictatorship.

**558**
Cyrus "the Great" becomes king of the Persians, a subject people of the Medes.

**550**
Cyrus, having organized the Persian army into a fearsome force, conquers the Medes and claims their empire.

**546**
Cyrus invades Asia Minor, conquers Lydia, then overruns the Greek Ionian cities.

**538**
Cyrus conquers Babylonia and then goes on to extend Persian borders eastward to India, creating the largest empire in world history up to that time.

**521**
Darius I becomes king of Persia and expresses the desire to continue expanding the empire.

**514**
In Athens, Hippias, one of the sons of Pisistratus, initiates a reign of terror, giving the word "tyrant" its modern meaning.

**512**
Darius leads an army across the Hellespont, launching the first Asian invasion of Europe; the Persians conquer Thrace, a sparsely populated region of northern Greece, as well as parts of Scythia, in what is now Bulgaria.

**510–506**
Athenian democratic leader Cleisthenes and his supporters overthrow Hippias and establish true democracy in Athens; Hippias escapes into Persia and takes refuge in Darius's court.

**506**
Athens intervenes in a dispute between its neighbors Thebes and Plataea, upholding Plataea's right to independence.

**499**
The Ionian cities, led by Miletus, throw out their Persian puppet rulers, initiating a widespread rebellion.

## 498

Athens and its mainland neighbor Eretria send ships and men to aid the Ionians; a raiding party of Ionians and Athenians burns the city of Sardis, Persian capital of Asia Minor; Darius swears revenge against Athens.

## 494

The Persians defeat a united Ionian force in the sea battle of Lade; Miletus falls to a Persian siege and the Milesians are killed or enslaved, marking the end of the Ionian rebellion.

## 493

Athenian leader Themistocles, recognizing the strategic importance of sea power to repel a possible Persian invasion, begins building Athens's port of Piraeus.

## 492

Darius orders his son-in-law Mardonius to lead an expedition into Greece to punish Athens and Eretria for their role in the Ionian revolt; Mardonius returns to Persia without completing his mission after much of his fleet is destroyed in a storm off the coast of Thrace.

## 490

Darius orders another expedition to Greece; the Persians sack Eretria and enslave its inhabitants; the Persians land on the plain of Marathon, intent on attacking Athens; a small army of Athenian and Plataean hoplites decisively defeat the Persians in the Battle of Marathon.

## 487

The Athenians initiate the practice of ostracism, or voting for the banishment of public officials, designed to keep any one such official from gaining too much power.

## 486

Darius dies and is succeeded by his son Xerxes, who continues his father's preparations for still another invasion of Greece.

## 484

Herodotus, the Greek historian who will later write a detailed chronicle of the Greek and Persian conflicts, is born.

## 480

Xerxes leads a vast army in an all-out attack on Greece; a small force of Greeks led by Spartan king Leonidas dies to the last man in the pass of Thermopylae; a united Greek fleet, led by Themistocles, defeats the Persian armada at Salamis; Xerxes retires to Asia Minor, leaving behind an army under Mardonius.

## 479

A united Greek army destroys Mardonius's forces in a major battle near Plataea; the Greeks defeat the Persians at Mycale in Asia Minor; Ionia regains its independence; thereafter, no Eastern power ever again poses a threat to Greece.

# History's Greatest Honor

As dawn broke on the morning of September 12, 490 B.C., the sun's first red-orange rays glinted off the polished surfaces of thousands of round bronze shields. The shields rested with bottoms on the ground and tops against the left sides of thousands of heavily armored infantry troops, or hoplites, from the Greek city-state of Athens. In their right hands the hoplites grasped the shafts of their sharpened spears, which for the moment they held upright, butt-ends in the dirt. The men stood silently, their expressions grim. Their well-ordered ranks stretched in a long line across one side of the flat, open plain of Marathon on the coast of the Attic Peninsula in eastern Greece. Uppermost in the men's minds was the knowledge that Athens lay only twenty-six miles away on the opposite side of the peninsula. There resided their families, friends, traditions—indeed, their entire way of life. That way of life faced the threat of total annihilation. For that reason the hoplite commander had told them earlier in a heart-stirring speech that they must stop the enemy here at Marathon at all costs.

That enemy now faced the Greeks about a mile away across the plain. Lining the seacoast in the distance was a vast assemblage of troops—the invasion forces of the Persian Empire, a huge and mighty realm centered in the arid lands north and east of the Persian Gulf in western Asia. The Persian warriors, rumored to be fearsome and invincible fighters, had but one aim—to conquer Athens. Once Athens, one of the foremost of the Greek states, had been taken, a larger invasion force would follow and overrun the rest of Greece. The Persians, leaders and soldiers alike, were confident of victory. All of the armies they had faced during many years of conquest had fallen before them. In fact, many peoples had been so afraid of the formidable Persian war machine that they had simply given up without a fight and submitted to Persian rule. Surely the situation would be little different with these Athenians, the Persians reasoned. Scouts had confirmed that the Greek hoplites were outnumbered four to one and had neither archers nor cavalry to back up their infantry. It looked to be another easy victory for the Persian army.

As the sun rose higher above the hills backing the plain, the Greeks waited tensely for the signal to begin the advance toward the enemy. They realized that their courage and skill in the coming battle would forever decide the fate, not only of Athens, but of all of Greece. What they could not have realized at the time was that this first great decisive battle in recorded history would profoundly shape the future of all of Western, or European-based, civilization. It would prove to be the first of many epic clashes between Western culture and its Eastern, or Asian-based,

*The Greeks, in their traditional phalanx formation (right) face the formidable Persian army. The Persians were confident of victory, outnumbering the Greeks four to one.*

*The Greeks, vastly outnumbered, overrun the Persians in a display of fighting skill and determination.*

counterpart. On that fateful September morning, the outnumbered Athenian hoplites would do much more than save their farms, city, and customs. They would also fire the opening salvo in a great war, a monumental conflict that would in the end stop the East from absorbing the West.

The Greeks' victory over seemingly overwhelming odds in that conflict would, in the words of historian Michael Grant, fill them "with immeasurable confidence about their own potential . . . and their future." Their deeds would also confirm their "powerful conviction of the difference and distinction between Greeks and [foreigners] and an assurance that the former, free men and members of free communities, were superior to the latter." In addition, the Greek warriors' deeds would awe and inspire later generations of Western peoples, becoming one of the most hallowed and glorious episodes in humanity's collective memory. In life, the Greek heroes of Marathon would receive the heartfelt gratitude and praises of their countrymen. In death, history would bestow upon them an even higher honor, and by far its greatest—everlasting glory.

# CHAPTER ONE

# West Versus East: Two Cultures in Collision

The first two decades of the fifth century B.C. marked one of the great turning points in world history. These were the years of the Greek and Persian wars, a struggle that pitted what was then the highest culture in Europe against the most powerful culture in Asia. This mighty confrontation between West and East was undoubtedly inevitable. As they grew and prospered, Greek and Persian spheres of influence eventually made contact along the shores of the eastern Mediterranean Sea.

Peaceful coexistence between the two peoples was out of the question from the start. For one thing, their backgrounds, customs, political systems, and goals were markedly different. There was also the problem of disputed territory. At first, this constituted the lands of Asia Minor, or what is now Turkey, especially its western coasts and islands, an area then known as Ionia. In time, however, the struggle widened across the Aegean Sea, the Mediterranean inlet separating Asia Minor from Greece, and into mainland Greece itself. The tiny Aegean soon became a bloody crossroad over which passed vast Eastern armies bent on conquering Europe. The events of the Greek and Persian wars trace the story of how some smaller but extremely determined Western armies, including the bold Athenian band at Marathon, prevented that conquest.

*Greek historian Herodotus believed that conflict between the Persians and Greeks was inevitable.*

## Reaching into the Dim Past

In a way, the epic Greek-Persian confrontation was many centuries in the making. The separate and unique ways in which the two cultures developed virtually ensured that their eventual

*The Trojan Horse hides within its bowels Greek soldiers ready to jump out once they enter the walls of Troy. Herodotus cited the Trojan War as the source of enmity between East and West.*

meeting would erupt into conflict. This was certainly the way the fifth-century B.C. Greek historian Herodotus viewed it. In his *Histories*, a detailed account of the background and events of the Greek and Persian wars, he wrote of "the perpetual enmity [hostility] of the Grecian world towards" the Asian peoples belonging to the Persian Empire. The Greeks, said Herodotus, drew a clear distinction between West and East. They saw "Asia with its foreign-speaking peoples belonging to the Persians, [and] Europe and the Greek states being . . . quite separate and distinct from them."

To Herodotus, the ways in which the two cultures became so separate and distinct was of paramount importance. The purpose of his book, he said, was "to preserve the memory of the past by putting on record the astonishing achievements both of our own and of other peoples; and more particularly, to show how they came into conflict." To do this, he began his story in the dim past, long before the Persian Empire and the Greece he knew existed. The first confrontation between West and East, he wrote, was the Trojan War. In this conflict, the early Greeks, who by Herodotus's time had become legendary heroes, laid siege to and sacked the prosperous trading city of Troy on the northwestern coast of Asia Minor. Centuries later, these events were immortalized in the epic poem the *Iliad*, traditionally credited to a traveling Greek poet named Homer. The Persians, said Herodotus, saw the Trojans as being among their remote ancestors. And so, in the Persian view, "it was the capture of Troy that first made them enemies of the Greeks."

## The Dorian Invasion

Historians now refer to the early Greeks who sacked Troy as the Mycenaeans, after their fortress-city of Mycenae in southeastern Greece. At the time of the Trojan War—about 1200 B.C.—the prosperous Mycenaeans controlled mainland Greece and the Aegean islands and frequently raided the coasts of Asia Minor. Their targets, including Troy, were mainly small independent kingdoms and cities. At the time, the future Persian homelands that lay a thousand miles east of the Aegean were ruled by the Assyrians, a warlike people whose influence did not extend into Asia Minor.

About 1100 B.C., an event occurred that would have important consequences for the later Greek-Persian conflict. The Mycenaeans suddenly found their way of life shattered as a less advanced and very aggressive people known as the Dorians swept down from the heavily forested lands north of Greece. The Dorians looted and burned the Mycenaean palaces and cities and the Greek mainland fell into a cultural dark age. Some of the Mycenaeans managed to escape across the Aegean. They

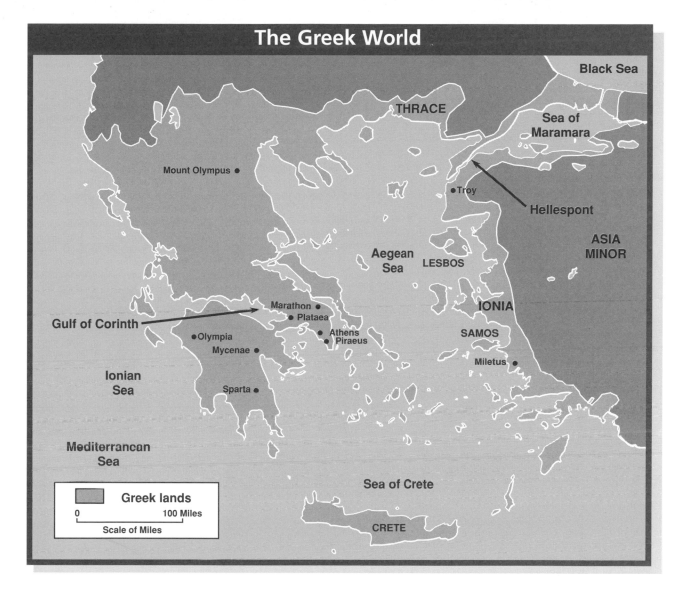

## The Greek World

settled on the coasts and islands of Ionia. The cities they founded, among them Miletus, Ephesus, and Teos, would later become the first Greek players in the epic drama with Persia.

## The Rise of City-States

During the three centuries following the Dorian invasion, Greek civilization reached its lowest ebb. On the mainland, in the Aegean islands, and in Ionia, the poverty-stricken survivors of a once powerful and prosperous culture learned to eke out meager livings as farmers, fishermen, and shepherds. Yet during these same years, they forged the unique Greek spirit of independence that would later infuriate the Persians. That spirit was a direct result of the growth of numerous highly independent towns and cities. All across Greece, small groups of people clung to their local valleys and islands in which separate societies evolved, each with a central township. This process, Michael Grant explains in his book *The Rise of the Greeks*,

> could happen in various different ways. A group of villages might physically amalgamate [combine] to form one township, as was the case, for example, at Sparta and Corinth [both located in the Peloponnesus, the large peninsula that makes up southern Greece], creating an urban focus for a previously scattered population. Or the villages could remain where they were and agree to accept one of their number as their center. . . . That is what happened in Attica, where the rise of Athens did not extinguish the villages of the territory but subordinated them to the new urban unit.

Most of the Greek townships were built around a central hill or cliff known as an acropolis, which means "high place of the city" in Greek. People used their acropolis as both a defensive position when attacked and a public and religious meeting area. But though physically similar, these townships developed their own distinct traditions and so came to think of themselves as separate nations. Thus a new kind of political unit came into

*The Acropolis at Athens is surrounded by temples and private residences. Most Greek poleis had their own, though less imposing, acropoli.*

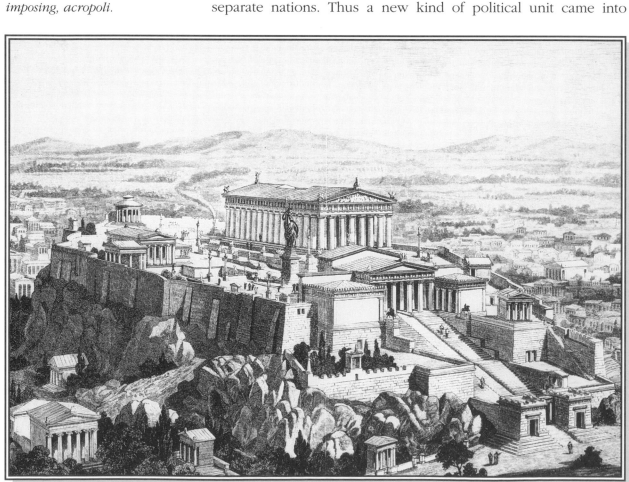

being—the city-state, a nation built around a single city. The Greeks called these tiny independent city-states poleis, each single polis consisting of the central town and its surrounding villages and farmlands. Even at the height of their development the largest poleis had a population of only about two hundred thousand people. Most had far fewer than twenty thousand inhabitants. In times of war, the large poleis usually fielded armies of only a few thousand men, while the average polis fielded no more than a few hundred.

Since the Greek poleis developed highly individual identities, the concept of individualism grew strong in Greece. Each city-state saw itself as having unique qualities worthy of respect. In time, that idea began to apply to the individual citizens of these states. Farmers, craftspeople, and other everyday people started to see themselves as being just as worthy as their leaders. At first, as in other parts of the ancient world, these leaders were kings, each of whom dictated the rules of his own state. But by the eighth century B.C., as Greece emerged from its dark age into a new era of prosperity, the newly evolving spirit of independence brought waves of political change. First, in most poleis groups of well-to-do citizens, or aristocrats, banded together and threw out the kings. A group of several aristocrats then ruled jointly, a form of government called an oligarchy, meaning "rule of the few" in Greek.

## Athens Takes the Lead

Most of the Greek oligarchies did not last long. This was mainly because the living standards and social status of ordinary people rose enough for them to begin demanding their own say in government. They also demanded laws that everyone in society, rulers and subjects alike, would be bound by. In the seventh and sixth centuries B.C., says historian Victor Ehrenberg,

> political individualism developed out of the tensions of social life. . . . There was, on the one hand, the urgent demand of the ordinary peasants no longer to be the victims of the . . . [rule] of the aristocrats. . . . Oppression and injustices were causes of growing complaint, and the first remedy was the codification [compiling] of law. . . . In various parts of the Greek world laws were written down for the first time. . . . Hence eventually sprang the idea . . . that the community of the polis was based on the rule of law.

Athens, the largest and most prosperous polis, took an early lead in progressive political change, including the development of written laws to govern society. After eliminating their kings, Athenian aristocrats recognized the civil authority of a figure called an archon, or chief administrator. He and other archons

### Athens

All through the centuries following the Dorian invasion, Athens enjoyed a number of fortunate advantages that in the long run ensured its emergence as the foremost polis in Greece. First, it was the only major Mycenaean settlement that escaped destruction at the hands of the Dorians. Although over time the Athenians lost much of their former heritage and suffered various hardships during Greece's dark age, they had a head start over other poleis in the region's overall recovery. Evidence also suggests that Athens played a leading role in settling refugees on the coasts and islands of Ionia. This helps to explain the close ties between Athenians and Ionians in later classical times. Athens had other advantages, including the Attic Peninsula's large size and diverse resources, which allowed it to support a considerable population, amass mineral wealth, and carry on thriving trade relations with other city-states. As classical historian Michael Grant explains in his book *The Founders of the Western World,*

> Special assets, when they came to be exploited, included the silver of Laurium [in southern Attica], the marble of Mount Pentelicus [twenty miles northeast of Athens], and the clay of the River Cephisus [flowing just west of the city]. Anchorages on the sand beach of Phaleron [five miles south of the city] and within the deepwater inlet of Piraeus [near Phaleron] . . . facilitated maritime communications.

added over the years were advised and held in check by a council of aristocrats called the Areopagus. At first, the archons ruled as they saw fit. But by the late seventh century, the *demos*, or common people, had forced the state to codify a set of laws. An aristocrat named Draco (or Dracon) drew up the first laws in 621, but these proved too harsh.

Then, in 594, an archon named Solon introduced several important political reforms. "At the request of his countrymen," wrote Herodotus, he "made a code of laws for Athens." To make sure that the aristocratic Areopagus did not have the sole authority in creating any future laws, Solon also set up the Assembly. In its early form, this was a group of citizens with a limited but real say in suggesting laws and choosing or rejecting leaders. Nearly all Athenians agreed that Solon's reforms were fair to all sectors of society. Solon himself wrote:

> To the *demos* I have given such honor as is sufficient, neither taking away nor granting them more. For those who had power and were great in riches, I equally cared that they should suffer nothing wrong. Thus I stood, holding my strong shield over both, and I did not allow either side to prevail against justice. . . . Laws I wrote, alike for nobleman and commoner, awarding straight justice to everybody.

Thus, although Athens had not yet achieved true democracy, by the early sixth century B.C. it was well on its way to that goal. And the city set an example to other poleis, some of which instituted their own political reforms. Athens also set the standard for excellence in the arts and architecture, producing many fine temples, public buildings, stone sculptures, and handpainted ceramic vases.

## Sparta

To be sure, not all city-states followed the Athenian lead. Of those that did not, the most notable was Sparta, which kept its kings and maintained a conservative, regimented society built around military training and the art of war. By the time of Solon's reforms, Sparta had the most powerful army in the Greek world. As a rule, the Spartans distrusted change and avoided contact with most of their neighbors, whom they viewed as radical and unstable.

Yet even the Spartans recognized that all Greeks, no matter how different their governments and customs, had certain fundamental attributes in common. First, from the Peloponnesus to Ionia, they all spoke Greek and therefore could communicate easily with one another. They also shared the heritage of their distant ancestors' heroic deeds at Troy, as chronicled in the national epic the *Iliad*. Citizens of diverse poleis could look back

*Archon Solon laid much of the groundwork for the city-state of Athens to become a true democracy, including passing laws that would apply to everyone.*

*Although Greek city-states differed, they were united by a common cultural tradition. They believed in the same gods, including Poseidon (left) and shared many of the same artistic traditions, including styles of pottery decoration (above).*

proudly to an era when all Greeks stood united. Religion constituted still another common cultural link. All Greeks worshipped the same pantheon, or group of gods, led by Zeus, the chief god. Other gods included Apollo, the sun god; Poseidon, who ruled the seas and caused earthquakes; Aphrodite, goddess of love and beauty; and Athena, goddess of wisdom and war and the patron deity of Athens. Thus, while the Greeks had differences and often squabbled among themselves, the traits they shared gave the whole Greek sphere a cultural unity.

## Built on the Wreckage of the Past

By the mid-sixth century B.C., the beginning of Greece's "classical" age, this Greek sphere was made up of hundreds of separate poleis clustered mainly around the shores of the Aegean Sea. Nearly all of these states had become culturally vibrant and commercially prosperous. One reason that the Greeks had enjoyed steady growth and development for so long was that no outside power had hindered them. For a long time, the civilized world's large empires—Egypt in northern Africa, and Assyria and Babylonia in western Asia—had considered the tiny Greek cities unimportant. So these great powers had left the Greeks alone.

But in the years following Solon's reforms in Athens, a new and very dangerous power—the Persian Empire—arose in the East. The Persians built their huge state upon the wreckage of prior west-Asian empires. By the mid-600s B.C., the centuries-old Assyrian realm had grown weak and found itself plagued by rebellions. The Egyptians and Babylonians, who for a time had fallen under Assyrian domination, fought back, as did a number of other subject peoples. One of these peoples, the Medes, who inhabited the area south of the Caspian Sea just east of Assyria's capital of Nineveh, proved unexpectedly powerful. In 612, the Medes and Babylonians combined forces and attacked Nineveh. They destroyed the city and the once mighty Assyrian Empire quickly fell apart.

The Medes and Babylonians divided the Assyrian lands and for a time coexisted in peace. Nebuchadnezzar, the Babylonian king who ascended the throne in 605, married a Median princess and built for her the famous "hanging gardens of Babylon," later named one of the seven wonders of the ancient world. Meanwhile, Cyaxares, king of the Medes, began expanding his own realm. In 585, he moved west into Asia Minor, most of which was then controlled by a people called the Lydians. Great admirers of the Greeks, the Lydians interfered little in the affairs of the Ionian Greek poleis on the Aegean coast. But Cyaxares was bent

*A depiction of the Hanging Gardens of Babylon, considered one of the seven wonders of the ancient world. The tiered gardens were an amazing feat of architecture, completely self-contained and watered by large water screws turned by gangs of slaves.*

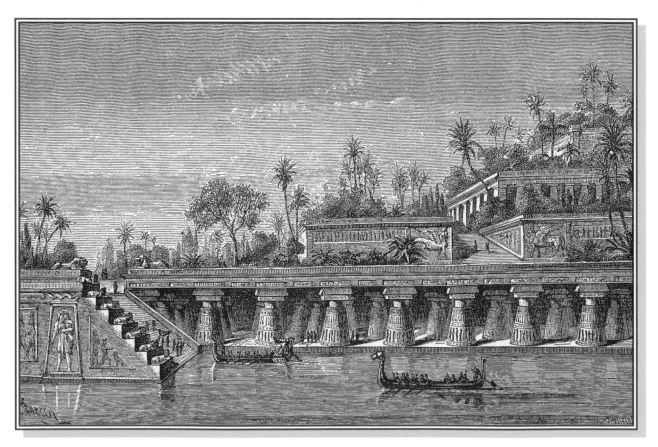

*Cyaxares (on horseback) tried to expand the Medean kingdom into Asia Minor. Luckily for the Lydians and Greeks who inhabited the area, he was stopped from attaining this goal by a solar eclipse—which he saw as a bad omen.*

on subjugating all the inhabitants of Asia Minor, Lydians and Greeks alike. Ironically, it was natural rather than human forces that kept him from achieving this goal. At the height of a great battle between the Medes and Lydians on May 28, 585 B.C., a total eclipse of the sun occurred. Believing this to be a warning from the Median gods, the superstitious Cyaxares marched his army out of Asia Minor, never to return.

In a way, the eclipse did prove to be an omen of bad luck for the Medes, for they were soon eclipsed themselves by a people closely related to them in language and culture. These were the Persians, who originally inhabited an area known as Fars, east of the Persian Gulf and southeast of the Median and Babylonian kingdoms. In 558, Cyrus II, later called "the Great," inherited the Persian throne. Acting on grand dreams of world conquest, he immediately organized a revolt against the Medes and by 550 had managed to take over the Median Empire. According to scholar Alessandro Bausani:

> The sudden rise and assertion of power of the Persians under . . . Cyrus the Great . . . is one of those astonishing but not infrequent phenomena in the history of Asia past or present. It shows how a tiny state can, for no apparent reason, trigger off an explosion like that of a new star, widely extending its boundaries to include many peoples of various races. . . . We have already seen an example of this process in the rise and expansion of the Median Empire.

# The Fountain of Law and Honor

One important key to Cyrus's success was a large, well-organized army. Regular soldiers in Persian armies came from the various lands under the king's rule. However, generals and other officers were always drawn from the Persian homeland so that the king could better trust his military leaders and advisors. The Persian soldiers wore brightly colored uniforms and carried a number of different weapons, giving them a formidable appearance. As Herodotus described them:

> About their heads they had soft felt caps called tiaras, and about their body tunics of various colors with sleeves, presenting the appearance of iron scales like those of a fish, and about the legs trousers; and instead of the ordinary [that is, Greek] shields they had shields of wicker-work [woven plant stems], under which hung quivers [of arrows]; and they had short spears and large bows and arrows of reed, and moreover, daggers hanging by the right thigh.

Well armed, well trained, and confident, the Persian troops quickly established themselves as the most efficient and feared army in western Asia.

Another key to Persia's success was its well-organized system of ruling conquered peoples. The Persians divided conquered territories into provinces called satrapies, each presided over by a satrap, or royal administrator. The satrap collected taxes for the king and dispensed local justice but had no military authority. High military commanders loyal to the king oversaw garrisons of troops and bands of secret military police who kept watch over each satrapy. This largely discouraged both rebellions by subject peoples and corruption by satraps and their staffs.

Overriding the entire system of armies and satrapies, of course, was the king, whose word was law throughout his empire. "In no [other] country," remarks historian Percy Sykes in his classic work, *A History of Persia,*

> has the national life centered more intensely round the king than in Persia. . . . The sovereign was the absolute master, the sole fountain of law and honor . . . the one man on whose character and capacity . . . the entire country depended. . . . The royal robe of purple worn by the Great King was the dignified flowing garment of the Medes, and on his head was set the high . . . tiara of bright color, which the monarch alone might wear. . . . He wore earrings, bracelets, chains, and a girdle all of gold, and appears in sculptures seated on an elaborately-wrought throne, wearing a long beard and curled hair. . . . A subject admitted to an audience prostrated himself [lay face down on the floor] on entering [the king's] presence and his hands remained hidden throughout [the audience].

*Ancient Persians dressed in typical, flamboyant garb. Here, a nobleman is flanked by two warriors, each wearing Persian felt tiaras on their heads.*

# Those Peculiar Persians

The customs and habits of the ancient Persians differed from those of the Greeks in many respects. Fifth-century B.C. Greek historian Herodotus, sometimes called "the father of history," recorded some of what he saw as strange foreign customs in his *Histories*, saying:

> The following are certain Persian customs which I can describe from personal knowledge. The erection of statues, temples, and altars is not an accepted practice amongst them, and anyone who does such a thing is considered a fool, because, presumably, the Persian religion is not anthropomorphic [having gods in human form] like the Greek. . . . Of all the days in the year a Persian most distinguishes his birthday, and celebrates it with a dinner of special magnificence. A rich Persian on his birthday will have an ox or a horse or a camel or a donkey baked whole in the oven and served up at table, and the poor some smaller beast. . . . When Persians meet in the streets one can always tell by their mode of greeting whether or not they are of the same rank; for they do not speak but kiss—their equals upon the mouth, those somewhat superior on the cheeks. A man of greatly inferior rank prostrates himself [lays flat on the ground] in profound reverence. . . . Themselves they consider in every way superior to everyone else in the world, and allow other nations a share of good qualities decreasing according to distance, the furthest off being in their view the worst. . . . Pleasures . . . of all sorts they are quick to indulge in when they get to know about them—a notable instance is pederasty [here meaning to have many lovers]. . . . Every man has a number of wives, and a much greater number of concubines [live-in mistresses]. . . . They have a profound reverence for rivers: they will never pollute a river with urine or spittle, or even wash their hands in one, or allow anyone else to do so. There is one other peculiarity which one notices about them, though they themselves are unaware of it: all their names, which express magnificence or physical qualities, end in the letter S. Inquiry will prove this in every case without exception.

*Unlike the Greeks, who built religious temples and statues as shown below, the Persians rejected such works, thinking them foolish.*

*Persian king Cyrus the Great succeeded in defeating the Medes. A Persian king had absolute authority over his people, and was treated as a god. This system was entirely different from that of the Greeks.*

## The Misery of the Masses

The Persian king and the small group of nobles in his court enjoyed lives of privilege and luxury that stood in sharp contrast to those of nearly everyone else in the empire. "When considering the ancient history of Asia," Alessandro Bausani points out,

> one should always bear in mind that expressions such as "the Persian people," "the Medes," or "the Babylonians" are only conventions which really mean "the few thousand people forming the ruling class of the states termed Persian, Median, Babylonian, etc.". . . The other classes of these states—subject classes . . . could pass indifferently from subjugation by one elite [ruling class] to that of another, with hardly any alteration in their basic conditions.

These conditions were almost invariably harsh. As was the case in most other ancient lands, the masses of common people usually lived in poverty and misery. Illiterate and barely able to keep themselves fed, they had no say in how they were governed and no chance for a better life for themselves or their children. Many social and political concepts that seemed perfectly natural to the Greeks were unheard of in Persia. These included the idea of individual worth, the ability to rise socially according to one's own merits, the freedom to speak out against one's rulers, and the equality of all social groups under the law.

Not surprisingly, in Persia, a land where most people were treated inhumanely, the gods lacked most human qualities. In contrast to the Greek gods, who took human form, made human mistakes, and often mingled among humans, the Persian deities were invisible, mysterious, and aloof. The chief Persian god was Ahura-Mazda, the "good" or "wise" spirit. He was involved in an eternal war with an evil spirit, or devil, named Angra-Mainyu. The faithful were expected to destroy the devil's creatures, which included ants, snakes, flies, frogs, and worms. In addition to such nondescript spirits, the Persians also worshiped inanimate objects and forces such as the moon, fire, and wind. In general, the Persian kings and nobles believed that the gods watched over and aided them, while to the masses of peasants these same gods often appeared distant and uncaring. The prevailing opinion was that the gods approved of the vast gulf between society's haves and have-nots.

Such distinct political, social, and religious differences between West and East—between the Greek and Persian

*Persian gods lacked many human attributes and were strange mixtures of beast and man. Below, a king worships the chief Persian god, Ahura-Mazda.*

*Persian society featured great gaps between the wealthy and the masses. Not surprisingly, the concept of individual worth was almost nonexistent to the Persians. Above, a Persian lady and her visitor sit in luxury while a slave looks on.*

spheres—mattered little before the two came into contact. When Cyrus the Great finally initiated that contact, however, these differences mattered a great deal. After subduing a number of former Median subject peoples, he turned his attention to Asia Minor. In 546 B.C., Persia's Great King set his fearsome armies on a collision course with the Lydians and Ionian Greeks. In ways no one dreamed of at the time, the consequences of that collision of cultures would echo through the entire Greek world and then down the corridors of history.

# CHAPTER TWO

# Crossing the Hellespont: Advance of the Persian Colossus

The immediate chain of events leading to the eventual showdown between Greeks and Persians on the bloody plain of Marathon began in 546 B.C. In that year, Cyrus the Great decided to expand his empire westward into Asia Minor, home of the Lydians and the Ionian Greeks. In attacking the Ionian cities, Persia penetrated the boundary of the Greek cultural sphere for the first time. It would not be the last. Cyrus's successors came to see the forested, sparsely populated lands of

*Cyrus the Great's attacks on the Lydians and the Ionian Greeks would ignite a series of events eventually leading to the Battle of Marathon.*

Europe as a fresh challenge, as new domains, potentially rich in gold and other resources, to conquer and exploit. To the Great Kings, mainland Greece represented a mere stepping-stone to these domains, a minor obstacle in Europe's doorway. Once that obstacle was removed, they reasoned, the Persians would continue on their destined quest to engulf the known world.

## A Mighty Empire Destroyed?

Such majestic ambitions require leaders with both military skill and magnetic, larger-than-life personalities. At least in the beginning, Persia had such a leader. Certainly, Cyrus proved his skills at military organization and maneuvers in his swift conquest of the Median Empire. And he projected a forceful, unstoppable, and often brutal personal image that struck fear into the hearts of his enemies. According to the ancient Greek historian Xenophon, Cyrus

> was able to extend the fear of himself over so great a part of the world that he astonished all, and no one attempted anything against him. He was able to inspire all with so great a desire of pleasing him, that they ever wished to be governed by his opinion.

With a leader of so formidable a reputation commanding such seemingly invincible armies, the Persian Empire had no trouble extending its borders. After consolidating the former Median possessions, Cyrus decided it was time to push those borders westward. He wanted to prove that he was a greater conqueror than Cyaxares, who, in Cyrus's view, had abandoned Lydia too easily. Persia's Great King, less impressed by omens than the Median leader, was certainly not going to let a mere eclipse stand in the way of his campaign of world conquest.

As the Persians entered Lydia in 546, belief in omens again played a key role in the unfolding events. This time, Lydia's king, Croesus, who greatly admired the Greeks and followed many Greek customs, consulted the oracle at Delphi, a town in central Greece. The oracle was a priestess who, the Greeks believed, acted as a medium between the gods and humans. People often traveled to Delphi to receive divine prophesies. Likewise, Croesus sent a messenger to learn whether it was wise to fight the Persians. The oracle told the Lydian king that if he crossed the Halys River and attacked the Persians he would destroy a great empire. So, filled with confidence, Croesus attacked. To his great surprise, Cyrus's army delivered the Lydians a crushing defeat, swept across the Halys, and sacked the Lydian capital of Sardis, located about fifty miles inland from the Aegean coast. As Herodotus pointed out, Croesus could not blame the oracle, because

*Croesus (far right) consulted the oracle at Delphi (above) about his upcoming battle with Cyrus. Croesus suffered defeat in spite of what he thought was a favorable, though ambiguous, prediction by the oracle.*

the god had declared that if he attacked the Persians he would bring down a mighty empire. After an answer like that, the wise thing would have been to . . . inquire which empire was meant, Cyrus's or his own. But as he misinterpreted what was said and made no second inquiry, he must admit the fault to have been his own.

Lydia's fall sent shock waves through the Greek world, especially nearby Ionia. The Ionian cities deeply regretted Croesus's defeat for two reasons, the most obvious being that he had always shown respect and friendship toward them. More ominously, they had unwisely refrained from helping him stand up to Cyrus. Now they stood alone, face to face with the mighty Persian war machine. In desperation, the Ionians appealed to Sparta, hoping that its leaders would take pity on fellow Greeks and send their renowned army to defend them. The Spartans, always reluctant to stray far from home, did not send their army.

However, they did dispatch a messenger directly to Cyrus with the bold warning that if the Persians dared to attack any Greek cities, Sparta would intervene. Insulted that such a seemingly tiny and backward nation would dare to speak to him in such a manner, Cyrus replied:

> I have never yet been afraid of men who have a special meeting place in the center of their city, where they swear this and that and cheat each other. Such people, if *I* have anything to do with it, will not have merely the troubles of Ionia to chatter about, but [also] their own.

## Ignoring the Logic of Unity

With Cyrus having called the Spartans' bluff, a Persian attack on Ionia seemed certain. At that moment, Thales, a leading citizen of Miletus, the largest and most prosperous Ionian city, called for the Ionians to unite against the common foe. As Herodotus told it, Thales advocated that

> the Ionians should set up a common center of government at Teos [about one hundred miles north of Miletus], as that place occupied a central position; the other cities would continue as going concerns, but subject to the central government, in the relationship of outlying districts to the mother city.

But like the Greek cities on the mainland and elsewhere, the Ionian poleis were fiercely independent and reluctant to unite, so Ionian leaders ignored Thales' suggestion.

Very soon afterward, as expected, Cyrus's forces descended upon and laid siege to the Ionian cities. The Persians were skilled in siege tactics, an art they had learned well from the Assyrians, and one by one the Greek poleis fell to the invaders. Two of these cities, on the brink of destruction, loaded their entire populations onto ships and fled. The inhabitants of Teos and its neighbor Phocaea sailed away and established new cities on the coasts of the northern Aegean and what is now southern France, respectively.

Not nearly so fortunate, the rest of the Ionian poleis suffered heavy casualties and complete defeat at the hands of the Persians. Some of the defeated Greeks hoped that their fellow Ionians had learned their lesson about strength in unity. Inspired by the Phocaeans' and Teians' daring sea escape, Bias of Priene, a city near Miletus, offered a suggestion that, in Herodotus's view,

> might have made them [the Ionians] the most prosperous people in the Greek world. The proposal was that all the Ionians should unite and sail for Sardinia [a large island west of Italy] and settle together in a single community; there, living

*Thales of Miletus wanted the Ionian city-states to unite against the Persian army. They ignored his advice at their peril.*

in the biggest island in the world, they would escape subjection, rule over their neighbors and be rich and happy. If, on the other hand, they stayed in Ionia, there was little chance . . . of ever regaining their freedom.

But once more, most Ionians ignored the sound logic of unity, with tragic results. All soon endured the humiliation of submitting to Persian rule as Cyrus installed satraps and military governors to control Ionia. The Greeks were forced not only to pay the Persians a yearly tribute, or large sum of money and other valuables, but also to provide men to serve as soldiers in the Persian military.

Meanwhile, Sparta and other mainland poleis did nothing to aid the Ionians. Even Athens, which had unusually close ties with Miletus and other Ionian cities, failed to help. The reasons for this inaction remain unclear. But it is likely that no one wanted to risk provoking an attack on mainland Greece by the reputedly savage Persians.

Satisfied for the moment with his western conquests, Cyrus turned his armies eastward. First, he attacked the Medes' old ally Babylonia, which, due to poor leadership, had in recent years grown weak. Its leading city of Babylon, located about two hundred miles west of the Persian capital of Susa, fell to Cyrus in 538 B.C. In the remaining years before his death in 530, the Great King continued to expand eastward to the borders of what are now India and China. Stretching from these lands westward some twenty-five hundred miles to the Mediterranean and Aegean coasts, and encompassing hundreds of different peoples, the Persian realm had become the largest empire in world history.

*Darius I gained power over the Persian Empire in 521. Darius, innovative and farsighted, wanted Persia to rule the world.*

## Justice Reserved for the Privileged

Yet, great as it was, the size of the Persian Empire did not satisfy its leaders. Cyrus's son and heir, Cambyses, turned south and conquered Egypt in 525 B.C. But three years later the new king died suddenly, either by accident or suicide, and for a short time it appeared that the Persian realm might fall apart. With no strong ruler claiming Cambyses' throne, several satrapics, including Babylonia, rebelled. In 521, however, Darius I, a member of the royal family, seized power in Susa and immediately set about crushing the rebellions one by one.

Once he had regained military control of the empire, Darius sought to tighten that control by reorganizing and better unifying the realm. He built a new system of roads connecting major cities, partly to enhance commerce and also to speed his dispatching of troops to potential trouble spots. The road from Susa to Sardis, now the capital of the satrapy containing the Ionian

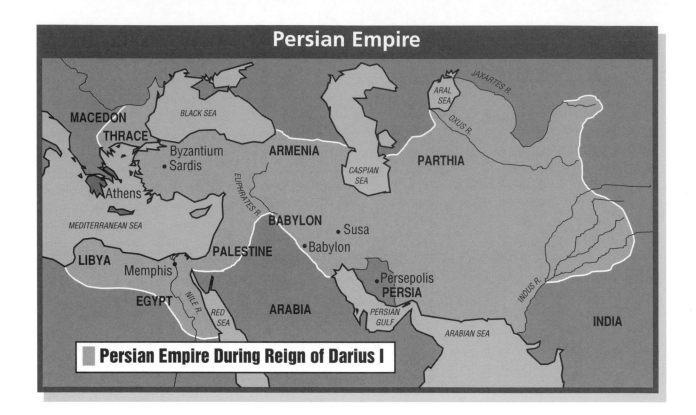

## Persian Empire

**Persian Empire During Reign of Darius I**

cities, stretched over fifteen hundred miles. A messenger on horseback was able to cover the distance in only fifteen days. Darius also divided the empire into twenty satrapies and assessed, or set the amount of, strict taxes for each. According to Percy Sykes, these provinces

> were assessed partly in money and partly in kind [food and livestock]. . . . Babylon . . . was assessed at 1000 talents [of gold, the equivalent of millions of today's dollars], and Egypt at 700 talents. . . . Darius was the first Persian monarch to coin money, and the "daric," a gold coin . . . was famous for its purity and soon became the only gold currency in the ancient world. . . . The taxes in kind were also heavy, Babylon feeding one-third of the army and of the court, and Egypt providing corn for . . . 120,000 men. The Medes furnished horses, mules, and sheep. . . . In addition, the provinces were called upon . . . to support the [local] satrap, his court, and army.

Darius saw himself as a fair man full of good and noble qualities. He himself summed up these qualities in the inscription he ordered chiseled on his stone tomb. "Says Darius the King," the inscription reads:

> By the desire of Ahura Mazda this is my nature: to that which is just I am a friend. I do not wish that the weak should suffer

harm at the hands of the powerful, nor that the powerful should suffer harm at the hands of the weak. . . . The follower after falsehood do I detest. I am not vindictive [vengeful]. If anything raises up anger within me, I restrain myself with reason; I am master of my emotions. Who works for me I reward according to his work. Who does ill I punish according to the ill he has done.

This self-evaluation was surely a distorted one. Darius, like his predecessors, thought nothing of subjugating and enslaving other peoples. Nor did he seem to view the servitude, starvation, and misery of large numbers of his own people as unjust. In the pattern followed by most other royal monarchs before and after him, he accepted that most people were inferior to the ruling elite and reserved the concept of justice mainly for that privileged class.

Certainly overriding any of Darius's ideas about justice and morality was his staunch belief that Persia's divine destiny was to rule the world. The faraway forests of Europe were a part of the known world that had so far remained untrodden by Persian boots. In 512 B.C., the Great King decided to remedy that situation. He led an army to the Hellespont, the narrow strait separating northwestern Asia Minor from Thrace, the sparsely populated Greek region bordering the northern Aegean. Darius's crossing of the Hellespont into Europe marked the first major Eastern intrusion into Western territory. The Persians proceeded to subjugate much of Thrace and several northern Aegean islands and then turned northwest. For many months, they raided the lands of the Scythians, a nomadic tribal people occupying what is now Bulgaria, finally halting at the Danube River. Then Darius, apparently satisfied with the first phase of his European campaign, marched south, spent a year relaxing at Sardis, and returned to Susa.

## The Continued Rise of Athens

Throughout Darius's campaign, the poleis of mainland Greece watched the Persians carefully and with great apprehension. The Great King had not chosen to invade south of Thrace this time around but many Greeks were convinced that such an invasion would come sooner or later. If so, who would lead the defense of Greece? The Spartans were the best fighters, but their failure to help Ionia in its hour of need showed that they could not always be counted on in a crisis. So, many of the smaller poleis looked to Athens, which, during the years of Persia's domination, had continued to cement its position as Greece's commercial and cultural leader.

In fact, the Athenians were particularly disturbed by the Persian takeover of Thrace because it gave Darius partial control of the sea route into the Black Sea. This made it more difficult for

## Darius's Engineering Marvel

While a ruthless conqueror, Persia's Darius I was also a prodigious builder. In addition to his ambitious system of roads linking the far corners of his empire, he also constructed whole towns and a magnificent new palace in Persepolis, another Persian capital located about five hundred miles southeast of Susa. Perhaps the most impressive of Darius's creations, and yet the least known today, was an Egyptian canal connecting the Nile River to the Red Sea. This waterway, which opened a shipping route from the Mediterranean Sea to the Indian Ocean and Persian Gulf beyond, predated the modern Suez Canal linking these same seas by almost twenty-five hundred years. Proud of his achievement, the Great King erected five stelae, or stone monuments, near the canal, bearing the inscription:

> Says Darius the King: I am a Persian. From Persia I conquered Egypt. I ordered that this canal be dug from the river which is called Nile, which flows into Egypt, to the sea which goes from Persia. Then the canal was dug as I commanded, and ships sailed from Egypt through this canal to Persia, according to my will.

In time, as the Persian Empire crumbled, the canal fell into disrepair and Egypt's eternally shifting sands slowly erased all traces of this ancient engineering marvel.

Athens to import grain from Greek colonies lining the fertile shores of that warm inland waterway. Attica's arid soil was good for growing grapes and olives but not for grain. Athens, therefore, with a population of over one hundred thousand and still growing, had for many years relied on the Black Sea grain connection.

The Athenians had gained solid control over the grain route at about the same time that Cyrus the Great had taken the Persian throne and begun his conquests. In 561 B.C., a year before the death of the great lawgiver Solon, Pisistratus, Solon's son and a popular military general, seized the acropolis and took control of Athens. He believed that certain aristocratic elements in society threatened his father's democratic reforms. Pisistratus's aim was to ensure the city's continued commercial and political growth. One of his first important acts was to secure the Athenian lifeline to the Black Sea, and by 556 his troops controlled the coasts on both sides of the Hellespont.

This was only one way that Pisistratus's rule helped Athens's continued rise to prosperity and greatness. Despite his title of *tyrannos*, or tyrant, he was not a cruel dictator, for at the time

*The Greek city of Athens, viewed from the Acropolis. Many Greek poleis looked toward Athens for leadership against the Persians, who they feared would invade all of Greece.*

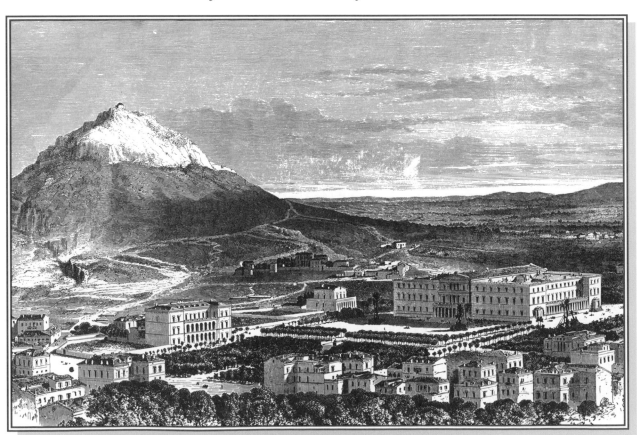

the term "tyrant" meant simply a person who held absolute power. Pisistratus used that power to uphold his father's laws and promote cultural activities, including literature, drama, and architecture. As Michael Grant comments:

> In spite of the subsequent prejudice against "tyrants," it was admitted, even by good later democrats, that the rule of Pisistratus could be looked back upon as a Golden Age. He had prudently refrained . . . from disturbing the existing Solonian constitution [set of laws], or from otherwise encouraging any major social upheaval, and the effective financial policy, which was his creation, had enabled him to stimulate national festivals, build temples and conduct a foreign program of bold expansion and skillful diplomacy.

## Victory over Tyranny

Pisistratus died in 527, about the time that, a thousand miles to the east, Cyrus's son Cambyses was preparing to invade Egypt. Hipparchus and Hippias, Pisistratus's sons, inherited their father's power. They ruled jointly for several years, continuing his enlightened political and cultural policies. But in 514, Hipparchus was assassinated in a private quarrel that had nothing to do with these policies. The assassins also tried, but failed, to kill Hippias, who thereafter became bitter and vengeful. He began a reign of terror that gave the word "tyrant" the meaning it has had ever since. Thus in 512, when Darius was leading his armies across the Hellespont into Europe, the Athenians had two major worries. One was the Persian threat to the grain route; the other was the menace of harsh dictatorship at home.

But Hippias soon found that his tyranny was no match for the righteous wrath of the freedom-loving Athenians. Between 510 and 506, an aristocrat named Cleisthenes, aided by Spartan troops, drove Hippias out of Athens and reestablished the rule of law in the polis. In fact, Cleisthenes and his supporters went far beyond previous reformers. They greatly increased the powers of the citizen Assembly, giving every free adult male the right to speak out and to vote. They also created the Council, a group of five hundred citizens chosen each year by lot, to formulate new laws and policies. The Assembly debated and voted upon the Council's recommendations. In free yearly elections, the citizenry chose three archons to run the government and ten military generals, the *strategoi*, to command the army. Thus, as the sixth century B.C. drew to a close, Athens created the world's first true democracy. Meanwhile, the disgruntled Hippias, insisting that the democrats had ruined the state, turned traitor and took refuge in Darius's court. Hippias's desire for revenge would later lead to his playing a key role in the Athenian-Persian confrontation at Marathon.

# Death Rather than Surrender

It is likely that the militaristic Spartans descended directly from the warlike Dorians who overran Greece at the beginning of the twelfth century B.C. In the eighth and seventh centuries, the Spartans evolved their famous system of training soldiers, one much harsher than in other city-states. This system soon gave Sparta the finest, most feared standing army in the Greek world. Only two groups were allowed the privilege of becoming Spartan hoplites. The first was made up of Spartan citizens, those adult males born in Sparta, and the second of *perioikoi*, or "neighbors," free tradesmen of foreign birth living in Sparta.

Only the strong could become Spartan soldiers. State officials examined male babies and any with birth defects or simply deemed too weak were "exposed," or left outside to die. Young boys had to leave home for state-run barracks, where they lived and trained in an atmosphere of rigid discipline and denial of normal everyday comforts, which have been called "spartan" conditions ever since. "For the most part," explains Peter Connolly in *The Greek Armies*, the boys "went barefoot and naked . . . to make them stronger and tougher. Their food was always simple and scant, so that they would be encouraged to steal. Although children were punished when they were caught stealing, the punishment was for being caught, not for stealing. This was to train the boys, so that as soldiers they might be able to endure famine and forage for themselves."

The young men had to endure this life until they were at least in their twenties and most were not allowed to marry until they were thirty. Even many of those who did marry and have children continued to live in the barracks and only periodically visited their families. A Spartan hoplite endured nearly constant daily training and exercise for most of his life and was expected to die fighting rather than surrender in battle. Spartan women were also expected to exercise and keep themselves in top physical condition, mainly to increase their chances of giving birth to strong, healthy boys for a new generation of soldiers.

*Spartan youths perform militaristic gymnastic exercises. Young male Spartans were rigorously trained to mold them into formidable fighters as adults.*

*A painting taken from a Greek vase depicts a hoplite. Hoplites made up the majority of soldiers in the Greek armies—they were not professional soldiers, but everyday citizens such as farmers and other landowners.*

Athens's victory over tyranny and its establishment of democracy filled the Athenian people with pride and self-confidence. The new Athens, stronger and more impressive than ever, became an example for freedom-loving Greeks in other poleis. And the Athenians took upon themselves a role they would play for nearly a century to come—that of champion of smaller states struggling for liberty. The first such instance occurred even before the democrats had completed their reforms. The tiny polis of Plataea, located on Attica's northern border, found itself threatened by its much larger neighbor, Thebes. In 506, Athens came to Plataea's rescue. An Athenian force met and defeated the Theban army and established Plataean independence. The grateful Plataeans would repay this favor in heroic fashion a few years later when the Athenians stood alone against the Persian onslaught.

# The Great Round Shield

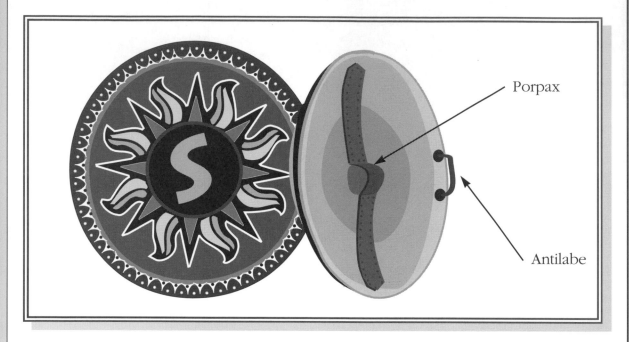

Porpax

Antilabe

*The markings on hoplite shields often denoted tribal units or had an initial letter or symbol to indicate the owner's city of origin. Common decorative themes included gods, demons, and animals.*

In this excerpt from *Arms and Armor of the Greeks*, scholar A. M. Snodgrass describes the piece of armor that most distinguished the ancient Greek hoplite:

The most important single item in the panoply [complete battle dress] of the hoplite, from which indeed he took his name, was the great round shield or *hoplon*. It was much larger than the round shield of the preceding era: the regular diameter is about three feet, and one exceptional example was found to be nearly four feet across. The shape is gently convex, except that the rim is usually flat. The basic material was wood, reinforced with bronze. The whole shield sometimes had a bronze facing. . . . On the inner side was a bronze strip, some-times short but more often running right across the shield, and bowed out in the middle to form a loop through which the left forearm was passed, up to just below the elbow. This arm-band, or *porpax* as the Greeks called it, was a new invention and peculiar to this kind of shield. At the edge of the shield . . . was a handle, the *antilabe*, a leather thong which was gripped by the left hand. This two-handled arrangement had many advantages: it helped to relieve the great weight of the shield, it enabled the soldier to release the *antilabe* if he wanted to hold a spare weapon without losing his shield, and it made it possible to hold the shield rigidly in an oblique [slanting] position so that the enemy's weapons would glance off it.

## The Rigid and Lethal Phalanx

For many Greeks, the small size of the armies that took part in the clash over Plataea underlined the enormity of the threat posed by a potential Persian attack on the mainland. Athens and Thebes were among the largest poleis, yet neither was able to field more than a few thousand trained soldiers. Even the Spartans had in the past rarely fielded more than two or three thousand men at a time. Yet for years, rumors had been filtering out of Ionia about well-armed and battle-hardened Persian armies numbering in the hundreds of thousands. If an invasion did come, would the Greeks be any match for such forces?

In addition to the issue of sheer numbers was the question of battle formations and tactics. Because no mainland army had ever faced a Persian one, Greek commanders could not be sure about Persian weapons use and strategies. The Greeks themselves relied on hoplites, or heavily armored soldiers, using bronze helmets and shields and six-foot-long spears. Most hoplites were not professional soldiers, but rather citizen-militia, farmers, and other landowners who could be called up to defend their polis on short notice.

The hoplites fought in a special formation called a phalanx, which had developed on the mainland in the late eighth and

*Greek soldiers take up the phalanx position. In this formation, the warriors formed an unbroken wall of bronze shields.*

early seventh centuries B.C. According to scholar Peter Connolly in his book *The Greek Armies:*

> The phalanx was a long block of soldiers several ranks deep. There were usually eight ranks, but there could be as few as four, or many more than eight. The phalanx was organized in files . . . so that when a man fell his place was taken by the man [in the file] behind. . . . This way of fighting was made possible by a . . . round shield, held across the chest [which] covered a warrior from chin to knees. When the phalanx was in close [tightly packed] order, the shield was wide enough to protect the unguarded side of the man on the left.

Typically, the hoplites marched at the enemy in this rigid phalanx formation. While the men in front rank jabbed their spears at their opponents, those in the rear ranks pushed at the backs of their comrades, giving the whole formation a tremendous and lethal forward momentum.

At the close of the sixth century, with the Greek phalanx as yet untested against the Persians, the mainland poleis faced an uncertain and perhaps dangerous future. Persian satraps and occupation forces lurked uncomfortably close in Thrace. And the threat of the Great King launching the next phase of his European campaign remained real. The Aegean sphere was like a powder keg waiting for a spark to set it off. Just as the new century opened, the Ionians supplied that spark. Sick of Persian rule and inspired by the recent triumph of freedom in Athens, the Ionian poleis made the fateful decision to rebel against their Eastern overlords. A drama of liberty versus tyranny on a far grander scale than the one just played out in Athens was about to begin.

## CHAPTER THREE

# Revolt and Revenge: The Fall of Miletus

After several decades of Persian domination, the Ionians finally gathered the courage to stand up to the Great King. Their rebellion against Persia, which began in 499 B.C., was an isolated and small-scale historical event. But as is occasionally the case with such minor episodes, the revolt set into motion a much larger and more important chain of events. What made the confrontation different from the one in the 540s, in which the Ionians had lost their independence, was that this time some of the mainland Greeks came to the Ionians' aid. For the Persian leadership, rebellions by subject peoples were nothing new. In such a huge, diverse empire, periodic minor revolts were to be expected and the military apparatus to deal with them was in place. What upset the Persians much more than the rebellion itself was the interference of the mainland Greeks. In the Great King's eyes, these culturally inferior outsiders had brazenly meddled in his affairs. And for that, they must be punished.

It is possible that had the Ionian rebellion not occurred, Darius might have delayed or even eventually cancelled his long-awaited assault on the Greek mainland. But as it happened, mainland participation in the revolt swiftly brought matters to a head and virtually ensured a vigorous new Persian thrust into Europe. The Ionians' brief fight for freedom, while itself merely a minor irritation to mighty Persia, proved to be the prelude to one of the most dramatic and decisive wars in history.

## The Right Person at the Right Time

The Ionian peoples had long dreamed of regaining their freedom. But as had been the case during their subjugation, they still had trouble uniting under common leadership, without which a rebellion would surely fail. In 499, the right leader at the right time arose in the figure of Aristagoras, a well-known citizen of Miletus. He inspired other Ionians, secretly organized them, and coordinated the first stage of the revolt. Suddenly and nearly simultaneously, all of the Ionian cities drove away or killed their Persian puppet rulers.

Aristagoras was well aware that this move would provoke an eventual Persian military response, so his next step was to seek help from the mainland poleis. Because Sparta's army was the strongest, it was the most logical first choice. Aristagoras hurried there to meet with Spartan king Cleomenes. At first, Cleomenes seemed responsive. The persuasive Aristagoras described how Persia was a land filled with gold, grain, and other riches, all ripe for the taking. The Persian soldiers wore trousers and cloth hats instead of armor, said the Milesian, and the Spartan hoplites, who were the best fighters in the world, could easily defeat

*Ionian Aristagoras went from one Greek city-state to the next in an attempt to persuade their leaders to unite against a Persian invasion. Since Sparta's army was the strongest (below) he hoped to persuade the Spartans first.*

them. But just when it looked as though Cleomenes might agree to an invasion of Persia, Aristagoras made a serious error. According to Herodotus's account, the king

> asked Aristagoras how far off Susa was, and how many days it took to reach it from the Ionian coast. Up to this, Aristagoras had been clever, and had led Cleomenes on with great success; but in answering this question he made a bad mistake. If he wanted to induce the Spartans to invade Asia, he never ought to have told the truth; but he did, and said it took three months. Cleomenes stopped Aristagoras from saying any more of the road to Susa. "Milesian," he cried, "you must leave Sparta before sunset. Your proposal to take Spartans a three months' journey from the sea is a highly improper one."

Aristagoras was disappointed, of course, but still confident about fulfilling his mission. His next stop was Athens and he correctly predicted that the Athenians would be much more responsive to his pleas than the Spartans had been. As Herodotus described it, Aristagoras made a speech to the Athenians, in which he

> repeated the arguments he had previously used in Sparta, about the good things to be found in Asia, about the Persian methods of warfare—how they . . . were easy to beat. In addition to this he pointed out that Miletus had been founded by Athenian settlers, so it was only natural that the Athenians, powerful as they were, should help her in her need. Indeed, so anxious was he to get Athenian aid, that he promised everything that came into his head, until at last he succeeded. Apparently it is easier to impose upon a crowd than upon an individual, for Aristagoras, who had failed to impose upon Cleomenes, succeeded with thirty thousand Athenians.

The elated Aristagoras returned to his homeland with the exciting news that Athens had agreed to aid the rebels. Moreover, Eretria, an Athenian ally located on the large island of Euboea, north of Attica, had also agreed to help. The Ionians eagerly prepared for a full scale revolt and to fight the Persians on land before they could mount any sieges against the coastal cities. But at that moment a prominent Milesian citizen, Hecataeus the geographer, urged caution. He argued that the Ionian strategy was all wrong. Insisting that sea power was the key to success, he said that the rebels should first build a large fleet and secure control of the eastern Aegean. Otherwise, the Persians, who had several fleets, would just bottle them up in their harbors and cut them off from the mainland Greeks. But Hecataeus's stubborn countrymen would not listen. Just as they had once ignored Thales and Bias, they now ignored him.

## "Sire, Remember the Athenians"

A few months later, in 498, the rebellion began in earnest. All along the Aegean coast, Persian-controlled cities expelled the Great King's officials and attacked his military garrisons. The revolt even reached Thrace, where the Greeks of that region, emboldened by the Ionians' actions, ended more than a decade of Persian control. After the arrival of twenty ships from Athens and five from Eretria, all loaded with soldiers and supplies, the rebels decided to show Darius they meant business. Aristagoras led a small raiding party of Milesians and Athenians in a lightning attack on Sardis, the Persians' principal city in Asia Minor. During the raid, Herodotus reported:

> One house was set alight by a soldier, and flames rapidly spread until the whole town was ablaze. The outlying parts were all burning, so the native Lydians and such Persians as were there, caught in a ring of fire and unable to get clear of the town, poured into the market-square . . . where they were forced to stand on their defense. . . . The Ionians, seeing some of the enemy defending themselves, and others approaching in large numbers, then became alarmed and withdrew.

Unprepared to fight a major battle, the raiders hurried back toward the Aegean coast. That they had not weighed all the possible consequences of the attack became clear when they saw a much larger Persian force pursuing them. The battle-hardened Persian garrisons stationed near Sardis had been biding their time, waiting for reinforcements from the east before dealing with the rebels. But now, in response to the attack on Sardis, they swung into action and caught up with the fleeing Greeks near the coast. The raiders, frightened and outnumbered, were quickly overwhelmed and suffered heavy casualties. While the survivors escaped to their respective cities, the Athenian and Eretrian commanders decided that their own best strategy was to return to Greece while they still could. Thus, despite Aristagoras's fervent appeals, the mainlanders abandoned Ionia to fight its own battles.

But if Athens and Eretria thought that withdrawing from the conflict at this early stage would prevent Persian counterattacks against them, they were mistaken. Contradicting his claim in his tomb inscription that he was not a vindictive person, the burning of Sardis filled Darius with the desire for revenge, particularly against the Athenians and Eretrians. When he had finished putting down the Ionian rebellion, he vowed, he would soundly punish the upstart mainlanders. Herodotus recalled how Darius demanded to know

> who, and what manner of men the Athenians were [to dare to defy him]. And when he had been told, he called for his

bow; and having taken it, and placed an arrow on the string, he let the arrow fly toward heaven; and as he shot it into the air, he said, "Oh! Supreme God, grant me that I may avenge myself on the Athenians." And when he had said this, he appointed one of his servants to say to him every day as he sat at meat [supper], "Sire, remember the Athenians."

## Disaster in Ionia

In the following four years, Darius slowly surrounded and over-came the rebellious Ionian poleis. Just as Hecataeus had predict-ed, the Great King's fleets seized control of the eastern Aegean, trapping the Ionians between the sea and the Persian land armies. The rebels fought back, often gallantly, but their cause became increasingly hopeless. Too late, they recognized the importance of sea power and in 494 B.C. made a last-ditch attempt to defeat the Persian armada. The huge Persian fleet approached the tiny island of Lade, not far from Miletus. "Presently, the Ionian fleet began to arrive," wrote Herodotus,

> and the ships took station in the following order: at the east-ern end of the line were 80 vessels from Miletus; next to them came 12 from Priene and 3 from Myus, then 17 from Teos, and 100 from Chios. The contingent from Erythrae and Phocaea followed, consisting of 8 and 3 vessels respectively; and next to these lay the Lesbian contingent [from the island of Lesbos], 70 strong. Finally, on the western end of the line were 60 vessels from Samos—making a grand total of 353 triremes [warships], against the 600 which the Persians had at their disposal.

The battle of Lade quickly turned into a disaster for the Ionians. For reasons unknown, just as the fighting began, forty-nine of the ships from Samos hoisted their sails, which were normally low-ered during battle, and fled. The remaining eleven Samosian ves-sels resolutely held their positions, but the Lesbians and several others panicked and swiftly followed the retreating Samosians. That left the ships from Miletus and Chios to face the main thrust of the Persian attack. Though these Ionians fought bravely, they rapidly found themselves overwhelmed. A few of the Chians escaped but were slaughtered soon after landing on shore.

The great city of Miletus was now nearly defenseless against the victorious Persians. The Milesians found themselves in a deadly vise, squeezed by enemy ships on one side and an army with siege equipment on the other. The Persians dug tunnels under the city's defensive walls and also used huge rams to bat-ter down both walls and entrance gates. Then they swarmed inside, burned most of the houses and public buildings, and

## A Great City's Former Glory

Miletus, located at the mouth of the Maean-der River on the Aegean coast of Asia Minor, was the greatest of the Ionian Greek cities. The date of the city's founding is unknown, but Greeks, perhaps settlers from Athens or Pylos on the mainland, had established a thriving community on the site by at least 1000 B.C. In the centuries that followed, the Milesians colonized the coasts of Thrace and the Black Sea, founding as many as sixty cities in all. These and other commercial ties made Miletus wealthy and prosperous and it became the recognized leader of Greek Ionia. Like Athens, the city also became a renowned center of arts and culture, featuring many fine temples, theaters, and public buildings.

After Miletus's tragic near-destruction at the hands of the Persians in the 490s B.C., it never regained its former stature. After the Greek defeat of Persia, Ionian refugees rebuilt parts of the city, but it always remained a small and very poor community, domi-nated first by the Athenians, and then later by the Macedo-nians and Romans. In time, Miletus's fine harbor silted up with sand and earth and the nearby island of Lade, site of the famed last stand of the Ionians against the Persians, became an inland hill. Eventu-ally, the town's inhabitants drifted away, leaving the majestic ruins that still stand as a testament to a great city's former glory.

# Masters of the Mediterranean

Most of the ships used by the Greeks and Persians in the Battle of Lade and similar sea fights were biremes and triremes. The bireme, introduced in the eighth century B.C. by the Phoenicians, a prosperous Mediterranean trading people, had two rows of oars, one above the other, on each side of the vessel. It also had a small raised deck on which a few archers and soldiers could stand during a battle. In the sixth century B.C., the Greeks introduced the trireme. This vessel had three levels of oarsmen on each side, making it faster and easier to maneuver than a bireme. Archaeological evidence indicates that a typical trireme was about 135 feet long, 20 feet wide, and could cruise at speeds of up to 10 miles per hour. Such a ship probably carried about 170 oarsmen, 20 or more other crewmen, and 10 to 40 soldiers during battle.

Just prior to entering a battle, the trireme's captain, or trierarch, ordered the mast and sails lowered and the ship then relied on the oarsmen to maneuver. At the time of the Persian Wars, the most common battle tactic for biremes and triremes was to ram an enemy ship. To this end, the bows, or fronts, of the vessels were reinforced with wood and/or metal, and covered with a large bronze ram. After successfully ramming another ship, archers fired arrows at the enemy crew. In the case of Greek warships, hoplites sometimes leaped onto the opposing ship and fought the enemy hand to hand. Biremes and triremes remained masters of the Mediterranean sea lanes well into Roman times.

*The trireme was fitted with three banks of oars. The rostrum, or beak in the bow, was used to ram enemy ships.*

killed almost all of the Milesian men. Some of the survivors, along with the women and children, became slaves. The Persians cruelly marched the others overland and resettled them in a remote desert town on the Tigris River in central Persia. Thus, by very nearly wiping Ionia's splendid leading city from the face of the earth, Darius both crushed the revolt and set an example to discourage the Ionians from future rebellions.

## A City Drawn Towards the Sea

When the news of Miletus's fall reached Athens, a wave of shock and grief gripped the Athenian populace. The people, recalled Herodotus,

> showed their profound distress at the capture of Miletus in a number of ways, and in particular, when [the playwright] Phrynichus produced his play, *The Capture of Miletus*, the audience in the theater burst into tears. The author was fined a thousand drachmas for reminding them of a disaster which touched them so closely, and they forbade anybody ever to put the play on the stage again.

Many in Athens felt guilty for abandoning Miletus so easily, while others insisted that leaving Ionia when they did had likely saved Athens from suffering Miletus's fate.

But one prominent Athenian was perceptive enough to realize that Athens had *not* escaped that fate. He was Themistocles, a brilliant young politician and military leader, who fully expected Darius to attack the Greek mainland. Like Hecataeus the Milesian, Themistocles recognized that sea power was the key to success against the Persians. In this view, with control of the Aegean Darius could easily ferry troops to the mainland and keep his land armies well supplied and reinforced. Sooner or later, reckoned Themistocles, the Persians would pound the Greeks into submission.

On the other hand, expanding Athens's tiny navy would give it the ability to destroy or at least drive away such potentially dangerous enemy fleets. But Athens lacked more than just ships. Located five miles from the coast, it did not even possess a sizable seaport with docks for a fleet of warships. So, in one moving speech after another, Themistocles, who was elected archon in 493, tried to convince the members of the Assembly to build both ships and ports. At first, he could get little money for ships. But he did manage to get permission to begin work on a port—Piraeus, on the coast south of the city. "And henceforward," wrote the Greek historian Plutarch,

> little by little, turning and drawing the city down towards the sea, in the belief that . . . with their ships they might be able

*Greek historian Plutarch (left) wrote about Themistocles' plan to build a navy to help repel the inevitable Persian attack on the Greek mainland.*

to repel the Persians and command Greece . . . from steady soldiers he [Themistocles] turned them [the Athenians] into mariners and seamen tossed about the sea . . . and bound them to the bench and the oar.

## Demands for Earth and Water

Only months after the Athenians began constructing the new docks at Piraeus, and even sooner than Themistocles had expected, Darius made his move against the mainland. Across the Hellespont and into Thrace marched an army commanded by Mardonius, the Great King's son-in-law. As Themistocles had predicted, a large Persian fleet slowly sailed along the northern Aegean coast, supplying and reinforcing the army. Mardonius's first order of business was to reconquer Thrace and punish it for taking part in the Ionian revolt. This he easily accomplished in only a few months. The next part of his plan was to march south along the mainland coast and punish Athens and Eretria. But late in 492, the fleet encountered an unexpected storm off the coast of southern Thrace. According to Herodotus, the

> violent northerly gale . . . proved too much for the ships to cope with. A great many of them were driven ashore and wrecked. . . . Indeed, reports say that something like three hundred were lost with over twenty thousand men. The sea in [that] neighborhood . . . is full of monsters [sharks], so that those of the ships' companies who were not dashed to pieces on the rocks, were seized and devoured. Others, unable to swim, were drowned; others, again, died of the cold.

For the moment, Mardonius's only choice was to return to Persia. The Athenians and Eretrians breathed a sigh of relief but their deliverance from the Great King's wrath was only temporary. Darius immediately began preparations for a direct attack on Greece, probably as a prelude to an even larger, more general invasion of Europe. For years, he had put his European plans on hold, and now, with revenge for the burning of Sardis his

*The ancient Greek port of Piraeus, which Themistocles built up in anticipation of a Persian invasion.*

## An Ambition for Distinction

Themistocles was one of the most brilliant and far-sighted Greeks of the classical age. Thanks to his forceful advocacy of building up Athenian sea power, he, more than any other single Greek leader, helped save Greece from Persian domination. In his famous biography of Themistocles, the ancient Greek writer Plutarch pointed out how, as a boy, Themistocles already displayed a powerful personality that later paved his way to positions of power:

> From his youth he was of a vehement [forceful] and impetuous [brash] nature, of a quick apprehension [wit], and a strong and aspiring bent for action and great affairs. The holidays and intervals in his studies he did not spend in play or idleness, as other children, but would be always inventing or arranging some oration . . . so that his teacher would often say to him, 'You, my boy, will be nothing small, but great one way or other, for good or else for bad.' He received reluctantly and carelessly instructions given him to improve his manners and behavior . . . but whatever was said to improve him in . . . [the] management of [his] affairs, he would give attention to, beyond one of his years. . . . It is evident that his mind was early imbued [preoccupied] with the keenest interest in public affairs, and the most passionate ambition for distinction."

top priority, the time seemed right to renew them. Darius had even more to spur him on than his dreams of conquest and his personal hatred for Athens and Eretria. Two former Greek rulers, now prominent members of his court, constantly urged him to invade Greece. One was Hippias, who hoped that the Great King would conquer Athens and make him tyrant there once again. The other was Demaratus, who had reigned with Cleomenes as one of Sparta's two kings. Having recently been banished by Cleomenes after a personal feud, Demaratus, too, hoped that a successful Persian invasion of Greece would restore him to power.

Darius's initial action was to intimidate the Greeks. Assuming that some would surrender without a fight, he sent messengers to every polis to demand samples of earth and water, a sign of submission. A number of smaller poleis, especially in the Aegean islands, were so terrified that they gave up at once. However, the reaction the messengers received in Athens and Sparta was very different. The Athenians sent them away, saying that Athens would never submit, while the Spartans were less diplomatic and more to the point. They threw the messengers into a deep well, calmly informing them that down there they would find plenty of both earth and water.

## Darius's Revenge Fulfilled

These defiant acts only served to increase Darius's desire to subjugate Greece, and this time he decided not to waste time marching an army around the northern Aegean coast. In the summer of 490 B.C., he ordered a military expedition, probably numbering about sixty thousand men, including sailors, to sail directly across the Aegean. The force was under the command of Datis, one of Persia's best generals, and Artaphernes, the Great King's own nephew. Their orders, reported Herodotus, "were to reduce Athens and Eretria to slavery and to bring the slaves before the king [Darius]." Hippias, now an old man, went along, confident that at last he would even the score with the Athenian democrats he despised.

The frightening news of the approaching Persian invasion force spread quickly through the mainland poleis. In Athens, some people muttered about how right Themistocles had been about sea power. If the Greeks had built a fleet to match that of Datis and Artaphernes, they would now have a chance of stopping the invaders well out at sea. As it stood, there was nothing to stop the Persians from landing their troops and ravaging the countryside. It soon became clear that the invaders had chosen unfortunate Eretria as their first target. "The Persian fleet," Herodotus recalled, brought up at [anchored near] Tamynae, Choereae, and Aegilia—all three places in Eretrian territory. The horses were immediately put ashore, and preparations for an assault began. The Eretrians had no intentions of leaving their defenses to meet the coming attack in the open; their one concern . . . was to defend their walls—if they could. The assault soon came, and there was weight behind it. For six days fighting continued with many killed on both sides; then, on the seventh [day], two well-known Eretrians . . . betrayed the town to the enemy. The Persians entered, and, in accordance with Darius's orders, stripped the temples bare and burnt them in revenge for the burnt temples of Sardis, and carried off all the inhabitants as prisoners.

By forcing upon Eretria a fate as disastrous as that of Miletus, the Persians fulfilled the first half of the revenge their king had dreamed of for eight long years. The victorious Persian commanders were confident that their second objective—the destruction of Athens—would go as smoothly as the first. Setting sail from Euboea, they headed for Attica. At this point, Hippias, who of course knew the country well, proved his usefulness. When

*The plain of Marathon, twenty-six miles from Athens, was the place the Persians selected to make camp before attacking Athens.*

Datis and Artaphernes inquired at which place on the Attic coast it was best for a large army to land and make camp, he told them about the plain of Marathon. Athens, he explained, lay only twenty-six miles away on the other side of the peninsula. Once disembarked at Marathon, the Persians would find the city and the rest of Attica easy prey. And with control of Attica, Darius would have a convenient and strategic foothold from which to launch more extensive European campaigns.

About the beginning of September in 490, Hippias guided the Persian ships to Marathon and the Great King's troops began streaming ashore. On hearing of this, Athenian leaders decided not to wait, as the Eretrians had, for the invaders to surround the city. It would be wiser, they decided, to try as best as they could to keep the enemy at bay on the coast. To that end, a small army of hoplites marched grimly but determinedly out of Athens toward the waiting foe and a stirring rendezvous with destiny.

# CHAPTER FOUR

# Attack at Dawn: The Bloody Clash at Marathon

I n the first two days of September in the year 490 B.C., the mood in Athens was somber and tense. Word had just arrived that the Persians, after sacking Eretria, had landed a large force on the plain of Marathon. That put the "barbarians," as the Greeks referred to Persians and other non-Greeks, within a day's march of the city. Athenian leaders quickly made two important decisions. The first was to appeal to the Spartans for help. It was, after all, in the Spartans' best interest to help repel the Persians, for if Athens

*A view of Sparta from the hills of Therapne. The Athenians hoped to get the Spartans to join them in facing the Persian army.*

*A relief depicts Athenian warriors as they march to Marathon in hopes of repelling the Persians before they reach the city of Athens.*

fell, Sparta was sure to be one of Darius's next targets. With the fearless Spartans at their sides, the Athenians reasoned, they might have a real chance of saving Attica and perhaps all of Greece. Time was short, so the Athenian generals sent Phidippides (or Philippides), a professional runner, on the 140-mile trek to Sparta in the southern Peloponnesus. He appears to have completed the trip in about thirty-six hours, an amazing feat considering that much of the route was very mountainous and rugged.

While Phidippides was on his way, the Athenian generals made their second and most fateful decision. This was to march the army across the steep Pentelicus range of hills to Marathon and try to keep the barbarians from moving on the city. Once the marching orders were issued, the army assembled in only a few hours. "The hoplites had their arms and rations ready," suggests Victor Ehrenberg. "Probably the army had been assembled ever since the fall of Eretria, which must have come as a great shock to the Athenians."

Large, anxious crowds probably watched and prayed for the departing hoplites, who ranged in age from about eighteen to sixty, as they strode out of the city gates and toward the hills. Some carried their armor and weapons in leather cases. Those who could afford it took along servants to bear both arms and supplies. According to Ehrenberg, they traveled to Marathon "either by the rough paths through Mount Pentelicum into the Vrana valley or . . . by the longer, but easier, road south of the mountains, which reaches the plain of Marathon from the south."

## Gratitude for a Valiant Gesture

After a march of perhaps ten to twelve hours, the hoplites reached the Pentelicus foothills facing the plain and began pitching camp. They could easily see the Persian camp about a mile away and the masts of Darius's ships perhaps another mile or two farther north along the coast. The great difference in the sizes of the armies was immediately apparent. The Athenians had nine thousand hoplites at most, while the enemy host numbered perhaps forty thousand archers and regular infantry, or foot soldiers. Supporting these Persian forces were about twenty thousand sailors, oarsmen, and laborers. Clearly outnumbered, the Athenians hoped that Phidippides would be successful in rallying the Spartans. For the moment, it seemed that the best strategy was to guard the road leading from Marathon to Athens and wait for help.

That help soon came quite unexpectedly from the north. Before the Athenians had even finished making camp, a contingent of about six hundred Plataean hoplites arrived. This was, in fact, tiny Plataea's entire army. Still grateful for Athens's aid against Thebes more than fifteen years before, the Plataeans had decided to stand, and if need be die to the last man, with their Athenian friends. None of the other Greek poleis had thus far sent help, apparently taking the shortsighted view that this was Athens's fight and not their own. Only the Plataeans seemed to recognize that the future of all Greece was at stake and that the only chance for victory lay in unity. Their hearts filled with gratitude, the Athenians never forgot Plataea's valiant gesture at this crucial moment. "Ever since the battle of Marathon," Herodotus recorded, "when the Athenians offer sacrifice at their [important festivals], the herald links the names of Athens and Plataea in the prayer for God's blessing."

Eventually, it became clear that the Plataeans would be the Athenians' only reinforcements. A few days after the Plataeans' arrival, Phidippides returned from his Spartan mission with disheartening news. As Herodotus told it, the runner had

> reached Sparta the day after he left Athens and delivered his message to the Spartan government. "Men of Sparta" (the message ran), "the Athenians ask you to help them, and not to stand by while the most ancient city of Greece is crushed and subdued by a foreign invader; for even now Eretria has been enslaved, and Greece is the weaker by the loss of one fine city." The Spartans, though moved by the appeal, and willing to send help to Athens, were unable to send it promptly because they did not wish to break their law. It was the ninth day of the month, and they said they could not take the field until the moon was full.

The Greeks at Marathon were well aware of how strict the Spartans were about observing religious laws. No doubts remained now that Athens and Plataea would have to fight the barbarians alone.

# An Appeal to Patriotism

As the two armies continued to face off across the plain, the commanders on both sides had some tough decisions to make. In the Persian camp, Datis and Artaphernes, who planned all strategy themselves, reasoned correctly that the longer they waited to act, the more likely it was that the Athenians would receive reinforcements. The Persian leaders certainly did not want to risk a showdown with the formidable Spartans if they could avoid it. Apparently, the Persians decided to take advantage of their superior numbers and divide their forces. The bulk of the army would stay at Marathon and destroy the Athenians and Plataeans, while a smaller force, including the cavalry, would sail around Attica and attack Athens. Thus, Datis and Artaphernes ordered the horses loaded back onto the ships.

Across the plain, the Greek leaders watched this maneuver with great interest. Their command structure was considerably more complicated than that of the Persians, consisting of both civilian and military leaders, most of them of roughly equal rank. As Michael Grant explains:

> Technically speaking, the Athenian commander-in-chief was a civil official, the polemarch Callimachus—the war archon, one of the . . . elected archons who were the . . . heads of the Athenian state. But in practice the command was jointly vested in the ten generals (*strategoi*), each elected from his tribe. One of these was Miltiades the younger.

At the time, Miltiades was the most popular of the generals. He also had the advantage of having once served in Thrace, where he had seen Persian armies in action. Therefore, the other generals, among them Themistocles and Aristides, another highly respected leader, deferred overall command to Miltiades.

To Miltiades, the removal of the Persian cavalry could mean only one thing—an assault on the city. In his view, there was no time to waste. The Greeks must go on the offensive and attack, despite their smaller numbers. Some of the other generals disagreed, so Miltiades asked for the support of the influential war archon, Callimachus. According to Herodotus:

> To Callimachus, therefore, Miltiades turned. "It is now in your hands, Callimachus," he said, "either to enslave Athens, or to make her free. . . . Never in our history have we Athenians been in such peril as now. If we submit to the Persians, Hippias will be restored to power—and there is little doubt what misery will then ensue: but if we fight and win, then this city of ours may well grow to preeminence [first place] amongst all the cities of Greece. . . . Yours is the decision; all hangs upon you; vote on my side, and our country will be free.

*Aristides, one of ten generals who commanded the Greek troops that met the Persian onslaught at Marathon.*

Faced with this strong and well-calculated appeal to his patriotism, Callimachus could do little else but agree, and the decision to attack became final.

## "We Shall Obey Our Leaders Unafraid"

Shortly before dawn the next morning, September 12, 490 B.C., the hoplites descended onto the plain and fell into their prearranged ranks in a large phalanx formation. Miltiades had ordered that the far left and right wings be the customary depth—perhaps eight rows. But he did not have enough troops to carry this depth along the entire battle line. He saw that the Persian line was nearly a mile wide and that he had to match this in order to keep the enemy from outflanking, or swarming around and behind, his army. So he thinned his long center to a depth of perhaps two or three rows of men. Following tradition, the hoplites were grouped according to the names of Athens's ancient tribes, and each general took charge of his own tribal unit. For instance, Themistocles and Aristides, who commanded the Leontis and Antiochis tribes, respectively, stood near the center of the phalanx where these units normally fought. Also following tradition, Callimachus claimed his right as war archon to command the right wing. The Plataean commander stood before his own hoplites, who manned the forefront of the left wing.

As dawn broke over the hills, the Persians had their first view of the distant Greek hoplites, arrayed in their full panoply, or battle dress. A hoplite's more than fifty pounds of armor and weapons consisted of a metal helmet topped with colorful horse-hair plumes; a thick leather breastplate, called a cuirass, that hung below the waist; metal lower-leg coverings called greaves; a three-foot-wide bronze shield; a spear; and a short sword, the latter usually used only if the spear broke. For the moment, to conserve their strength, the men rested their shields and spears on the ground. And for comfort they rested their helmets on the backs of their heads away from their faces. Looking out across the plain, they could see that the Persians wore little or no metal armor and bore shields of woven wicker. Yet despite this lack of body protection, their large numbers and wide range of weapons, including bows, short spears, swords, and daggers, gave their battle line a formidable appearance.

When the ranks were fully formed, Miltiades stood in front of the phalanx and signalled for some men to bring forth a goat. After a short prayer, he sacrificed the animal by slitting open its throat with his sword. He then examined the consistency of the blood and how it flowed in the dirt. Satisfied that the gods had sent a favorable omen, he next addressed the troops in a loud voice. His rousing battle speech has not survived. But he likely reminded his men that their actions in the next few hours would

*This drawing depicts hoplite battle armor, including bronze helmets, leather cuirasses, and leg greaves.*

*Miltiades led the Athenian troops in the Battle of Marathon. A popular general, Miltiades had previously seen the Persian soldiers in action.*

decide forever the fates of Athens, Plataea, and the rest of Greece. Miltiades now turned and began marching toward the enemy. Resting their spears on their right shoulders and maintaining their ranks, the hoplites followed. And as they marched they sang the paean, or battle hymn, designed both to steel their own nerves and to intimidate the enemy. Though the Athenian paeans have been lost, they must have closely resembled this surviving Spartan war song:

> We shall put all our trust in the gods undying,
>   And obey our leaders unafraid.
> And straightaway all of us shall stand together,
>   Posted near to where the spearmen are.
> Dread shall the din be when both charge together,
>   Striking rounded shield on rounded shield.

## Like a Ferocious Beast

The sounds of thousands of singing voices must have echoed across the plain to the Persians, who were surprised and confused by the Greek advance. According to Herodotus:

> The Persians, seeing the attack developing . . . prepared to meet it, thinking it suicidal madness for the Athenians to risk an assault with so small a force . . . with no support from either cavalry or archers. . . . Nevertheless, the Athenians came on.

As the Persian soldiers and their commanders watched, the Greek phalanx finally stopped at a distance of about 200 yards, the maximum range of the Persian arrows. Miltiades and the other generals walked back and took their places in the front ranks. Then, all the hoplites lowered their helmets into place.

Suddenly the battle trumpet sounded. At this signal, the Greeks, in near unison, lifted their shields into the defensive position and swung their spears off their shoulders, up, and forward. According to Plutarch, this swift phalanx tactic gave the formation "the look of some ferocious beast as it wheels at bay and stiffens its bristles." Such an unexpected and formidable sight must surely have struck fear into many of the soldiers in the Persian front ranks. A great silence now hung over the plain as the thousands on both sides stood very still and eyed each other anxiously. Scholar of ancient battles Victor Hanson describes how, seconds before such conflicts began, "an eerie quiet . . . came over the armies, as if the men had all suddenly been stunned, struck dumb at the very sight [of the enemy]."

Finally, at Miltiades' signal, a mighty blast of the trumpet broke the silence. The Greeks charged forward, screaming the Athenian battle cry—"Eleleu!"—as they went. "They were the first

*Miltiades leads his troops in the Battle of Marathon. The Athenians charged the Persians boldly at a full run.*

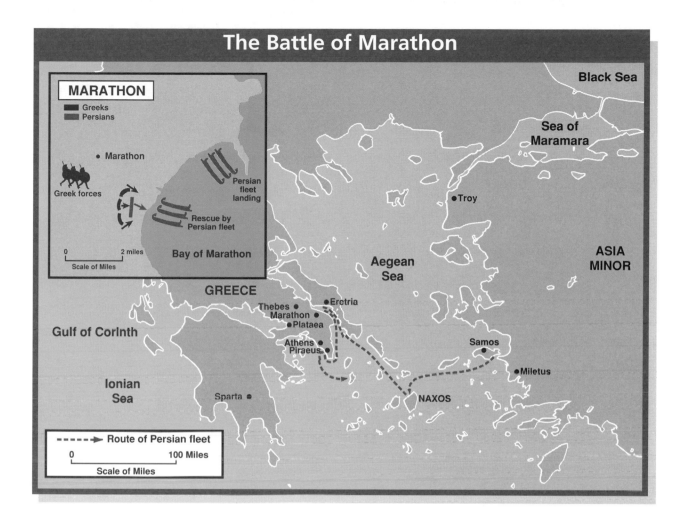

## The Battle of Marathon

MARATHON
- Greeks
- Persians

Marathon

Greek forces

Persian fleet landing

Rescue by Persian fleet

Bay of Marathon

0    2 miles
Scale of Miles

GREECE

Black Sea

Sea of Maramara

Troy

Aegean Sea

ASIA MINOR

Gulf of Corinth

Thebes
Marathon
Plataea
Eretria

Athens
Piraeus

Samos

Miletus

Ionian Sea

Sparta

NAXOS

- - - - ► Route of Persian fleet
0                      100 Miles
Scale of Miles

Greeks, so far as I know," wrote Herodotus, "to charge at a run, and the first who dared to look without flinching at Persian dress and the men who wore it; for until that day came, no Greek could hear even the word Persian without terror."

Hastily, the Persian commanders ordered their thousands of archers to fire, and a huge wave of arrows leaped up and outward. But the Greeks, trained for such an event, raised their shields and easily deflected the deadly barrage. Again the archers fired and once more the missiles had no real effect. The archers probably did not have a chance to fire again, for the Greeks had swiftly closed the gap between the two armies.

## A Devastating Impact

Seconds later, as the tiny but determined Greek army bore down upon the foe, the battle was at last engaged. In a great crash of metal on metal and the din of thousands of raised voices, the moving phalanx collided with the Persian line. The front Persian ranks staggered backward under the devastating impact of the

*The Greek phalanx. The Greeks had more than one battle advantage over the Persians going into Marathon. The fact that the Greeks fought as a single unit, unlike the Persians, who broke ranks to fight as individuals, was an especially fortunate advantage.*

charge and many Persian soldiers were immediately impaled on Greek spears.

On the wings, the superiority of Greek armor, training, and formation quickly became apparent. Once a battle had begun, Persian soldiers usually fought individually, that is, man to man. They were not trained for and could not stand up to the mass of bristling armor and great forward momentum of the eight-rank-deep phalanx. The wing formations moved relentlessly onward, like mighty steamrollers, mowing down the Persian front ranks. The men in these ranks were hemmed in by thousands of their comrades to their rear and so had no means of escape. Some who fell wounded soon found the enormous mass of the phalanx moving right over them. Hoplites in the rear files of the formation killed these crawling stragglers by jabbing downward with the sharpened "butt-spikes" on the rear ends of their spears.

Meanwhile, in the center of the battle line, where the Greek ranks were much thinner, the Persians were able, by their sheer numbers, to make some headway. They slowly pushed the Greek center backward and formal phalanx tactics largely gave way to regular hand-to-hand combat. Here again, though they were of necessity backing up before the enemy, the hoplites' superior armor and training made them more than a match for the Persians. According to Plutarch, "The main body of the Athenians being the hardest put to it [most overwhelmed by the enemy], the barbarians, for a long time, making opposition there [in the center] against the tribes Leontis and Antiochis, Themistocles and Aristides being ranged together fought valiantly."

## The Taste of Victory

Probably thinking that their apparent success in the center was a prelude to victory, the main body of the Persian army pressed forward vigorously. But they were unknowingly moving into the jaws of a trap that Miltiades had fashioned. The deep phalanxes on the Greek wings, having already annihilated the Persian wings, suddenly turned inward on the Persian center. Now hemmed in on three sides, the Persians found themselves trapped in a deadly vise. As the lethal phalanxes began squeezing them closer and closer together, the Persian ranks degenerated into a chaotic mass of confused and terrified men. Once the most confident and feared warriors in the world, they could think of nothing else now but escape. Their screams of fear and panic rising into a deafening roar, by the thousands they turned and fled. Many were crushed or suffocated by their own comrades as the irresistible wave of human flesh rolled toward the shore and the Persian ships.

Tasting victory, the Greeks once again raised their fearsome war cries and eagerly pursued the retreating Persians. "Here again," wrote Herodotus, the Greeks

> were triumphant, chasing the routed enemy, and cutting them down until they came to the sea, and men were calling for fire and taking hold of the ships. It was in this phase of the struggle that the war archon Callimachus was killed, fighting bravely, and . . . Cynegirus, too, the son of Euphorion, had his hand cut off with an ax as he was getting hold of a ship's stern, and so lost his life, together with many other well-known Athenians.

Witnessing Cynegirus's tragic death may well have been his brother, Aeschylus, who survived the battle to become the world's first great dramatist. The Greeks continued to slaughter enemy stragglers in the shallow surf until the remaining Persians made good their escape. A steady barrage of arrows from the ships probably made capturing these vessels difficult, and only seven fell into Greek hands.

A count of the dead revealed the enormity of the Greek victory. Over 6,400 Persian bodies littered the plain and the beaches, while only 192 Athenians had been killed. Miltiades ordered that the bodies of the slain Greeks be gathered together and also that a victory trophy be erected. This trophy, a wooden framework displaying captured enemy arms and artifacts, probably stood on the spot in the center of the battlefield where the Persian retreat began.

The placement of a victory trophy was usually accompanied by a celebration. But the Greek commanders informed their men that this time the festivities would have to wait. The escaping Persian fleet was heading south, apparently in an effort to sack Athens before the Greek army could get there. The exhausted hoplites would have to endure a grueling forced march over the hills in order to save the city.

In the meantime, Miltiades sent Phidippides on ahead of the army, to carry both the news of victory and a warning about the approaching Persians. Despite his fatigue after his recent run to Sparta and back and having fought all morning in heavy armor, Phidippides rose to the challenge. Pushing himself past normal limits of human endurance, he reached Athens in perhaps three hours, delivered his message, and then died shortly afterward of exhaustion. Centuries later, the modern Olympic Games introduced a "marathon" race of twenty-six miles, the distance from Marathon to Athens, in honor of this feat of strength and valor.

*The Greek hoplites rout the Persians, who run amok as they attempt to reach the waiting ships and escape.*

*The Greek messenger Phidippides passed into legend for his remarkable run back to Athens to tell the citizens of the Greek victory. The effort killed him.*

## Walking Among the Corpses

As expected, the Persians sailed around Cape Sunium at Attica's southern tip and made their way up the coast. But when they approached Athens, they saw more than the rugged Acropolis topped by its temples and statues looming in the distance. Not far from the shore, the very same army that had defeated them the day before was there to greet them. After crossing the hills at the double, the hoplites had formed another formidable-looking phalanx and were ready to fight another battle. This sight was enough to make Datis and Artaphernes think twice about attacking the city. They anchored their fleet offshore for a few hours, perhaps to make sure all of the ship captains received the newest order. This was to abandon the expedition and return to Asia Minor. It is likely that later that day when the last Persian sails disappeared over the eastern horizon, a massive celebration began in Athens.

## "A Tortured Symphony of Shrieks"

The peculiar, loud, and frightening sounds that accompanied ancient Greek battle must have impressed and haunted the participants, for several ancient writers described these noises. Here, classical scholar Victor Hanson comments on some of these accounts in his book *The Western Way of War:*

> The entire noise of men and equipment was concentrated onto the small area of the ancient battlefield—itself usually a small plain encircled by mountains, which only improved the acoustics [magnification of sounds]. . . . The *nature* of the sound also changed from that of recognizable human speech . . . to a terrible cacophony [din] of smashed bronze, wood, and flesh. Very early on in Greek literature we learn that the ancients were well aware of this particular inhuman sound of death. . . . [The Greek historian] Xenophon, in his famous description of the battle of Koroneia in 394 [B.C.] . . . was clearly impressed by . . . that "particular sound, . . . and then there was a great slaughter of men, and too, a great thud of all types of weapons and missiles, together with a great shout of men calling out for help among the rank, or urging each other onward, or praying to the gods.". . . The live sounds were more animal-like than human: the concerted groans of men exerting themselves . . . [and] there were all too often the noises of human misery. Here arose a tortured symphony of shrieks as a man went down with a wound to the groin, the steady sobbing of a soldier in extremis [dying], a final gasp of fright as the spear thrust found its way home. Ugly, indeed, [Spartan poet] Tyrtaios wrote, is the corpse in the dust.

Meanwhile, the full moon had come and gone. The Spartans, who knew nothing of the events at Marathon, finally went into action. "Two thousand Spartans set off for Athens," recalled Herodotus:

> They were so anxious not to be late that they were in Attica on the third day after leaving Sparta. They had, of course, missed the battle; but such was their passion to see the Persians, that they went to Marathon to have a look at the bodies.

This great desire to view the battlefield corpses was not unusual among the Greeks, or most other ancient peoples for that matter. Perhaps this was because of the particularly brutal and graphic results of thousands of men hacking away at one another with swords and spears. The sight of the aftermath of battle, though gruesome, must have been so unlike anything else in human experience as to be strongly compelling. Victor Hanson comments:

## How Far Could a Hoplite Run?

In his *Histories*, Herodotus wrote that when the Athenians charged the Persians the hoplites covered the entire mile separating the armies "at the run." Over the years, this statement has provoked a great deal of scholarly debate. Some historians have simply accepted the account outright, while others have expressed doubt that the hoplites could have accomplished such a feat. The doubters have maintained that a man carrying over fifty pounds of armor and weapons could not have run a mile and still had enough energy left to fight a grueling battle.

In the spring of 1973, some professors at Pennsylvania State University conducted an experiment designed to test Herodotus's statement. They chose ten young physical education majors in top condition and loaded them down with fifteen pounds of weights. Each athlete also carried a simulated shield weighing nine pounds, which he held up in an extended position with his left arm. The object was for the young men to run with the shields held chest-high for 1,600 yards, or about a mile.

The results of the experiment were revealing. Not a single one of the athletes was able to maintain the chest-high position for more than seventy-five yards and most were unable even to keep running past three hundred yards. Only one subject, a varsity long-distance runner, completed the whole 1,600 yards, but did so in a state of complete exhaustion. "Clearly," write classical scholars Walter Donlan and James Thompson, "Herodotus's account is not accurate." It is more likely, they maintain, that when the hoplites "came within effective bowshot range, something short of two hundred yards, they broke into a run, covering the dangerous distance rapidly, and closed with the startled Persians. . . . A generation or more of retelling obscured fact in a romantic haze."

Often a macabre [ghastly] fascination with the dead is illustrated in the many accounts in Greek literature where there are references to a postmortem [after death] "viewing" by a host of onlookers. Indeed, there was almost an urgent need to look upon the dead as they lay, before the bodies were carted away and the enormity of the scene was lost. . . . Of course, it was a standard practice for the victorious commander to view the dead, to examine closely the remains of those who had killed many of his own men and were now for the first and last time to be approached with impunity [in safety]. . . . Besides the sheer concentration of bodies, the most common sight to these onlookers would have been the quantity of spilled blood and gore. In some of the larger battles . . . thousands of corpses lay with huge, gaping wounds from the spear and sword. Since the flesh was never incinerated [burned] as it came to be in modern battles by the explosion of bomb and shell . . . the bodies would have

*Legend has it that the goddess Athena helped the Greeks win the Battle of Marathon.*

drained much of their body fluids upon the ground. Walking among the pile of corpses entailed treading everywhere over stained earth and pools of blood.

Satisfied with their inspection of the gore-covered Marathon battlefield, the Spartans "complimented the Athenians on their good work" and returned to Sparta. It must have been a somber homecoming. Surely, the Spartan leaders realized that in their tardiness they had missed more than a good fight. The glory for saving Greece now belonged exclusively to the Athenians and Plataeans.

## The Fabric of Legend

During the celebrations in Athens, many stories of danger and heroism on the field of Marathon were undoubtedly told and retold. But one story stood out from the rest in the minds of the deeply religious Greeks. According to Herodotus:

> During the action a very strange thing happened: Epizelus . . . an Athenian soldier, was fighting bravely when he suddenly lost the sight of both eyes, though nothing had touched him anywhere—neither sword, spear, nor missile. From that moment he continued blind as long as he lived. I am told that when speaking about what happened to him he used to say that he fancied he was opposed by a man of great stature in heavy armor, whose beard overshadowed his shield; but the phantom passed him by, and killed the man at his side.

Such ghostly apparitions had appeared in the legendary battles of past ages. In particular, the *Iliad* told of Athena and other gods interceding in the fighting and helping one side or the other. Had the gods been there at Marathon, ensuring the Greek victory? Epizelus's story seemed to confirm that they had. Thus, only days after the victory, the memories of the event had already begun to take on an epic and mystical quality. Over time, this process would continue as the real deeds of the Athenian and Plataean hoplites became increasingly interwoven in the eternal fabric of legend.

# CHAPTER FIVE

# Total Victory: The Greeks Make Europe Possible

The Athenian triumph at Marathon sparked joyous celebrations and prayers of thanksgiving across much of the Greek mainland. Having risked all and won, Athens had forever shattered the myth of Persian invincibility and in the process halted a foreign intrusion onto Greek soil. For this amazing accomplishment, the city received a vast outpouring of praises and gained immeasurably in prestige.

The weeks and months following the battle witnessed numerous tributes and memorials to the victory. Among these were bronze and marble statues and monuments at Marathon and in Delphi, as well as in Athens and other poleis. The Athenian government commissioned a huge painting covering an entire wall of a building in the city marketplace. This work, now lost, depicted a moment from the battle's height, with lifelike portraits of Miltiades and many of the other heroes, as well as images of the gods spurring them on. Writers penned heroic poems and detailed histories. Although the histories have not survived, some became the source materials for ancient historians such as Herodotus and Plutarch. The hoplites who fought in the battle became known as the "men of Marathon" and were treated as national heroes for the rest of their lives.

Although Athens had been the most commercially successful polis in Greece before the battle, in the years following it the city became even more prosperous. The Athenians took advantage of their status as the saviors of Greece by expanding trade relations and sponsoring cultural endeavors. People from many poleis traveled to the city to attend dramatic presentations in the Theater of

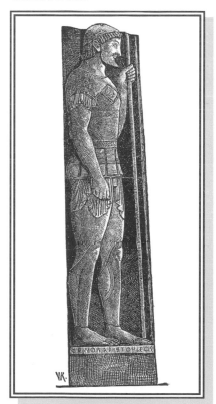

*A depiction of a Greek statue of a soldier at Marathon. Many such statues were built to honor the Greek heroes.*

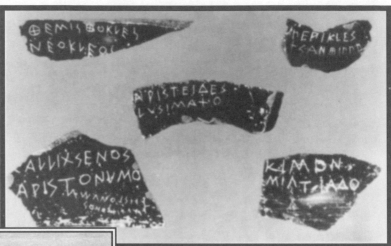

*In the years following the Battle of Marathon, the Athenians enacted several new changes. One was the building of the Parthenon (left) in honor of the goddess Athena. Second was the practice of ostracism, to banish unpopular leaders. Above are samples of the bits of pottery on which citizens wrote their choices for ostracism.*

Dionysus, which at the time sat fourteen thousand. And workers began construction on a large new temple—the Parthenon, dedicated to the patron goddess Athena—atop the Acropolis. The city also further expanded its democracy by introducing the practice of ostracism in 487 B.C. In order to ensure that no public figure could become too powerful, citizens could write the name of an official they wanted removed on broken pieces of pottery called ostrakons. If the official received six thousand or more of these negative votes, the city banished him for a period of ten years.

## Persia's New Leader

But while the Greek victory produced an outburst of commercial prosperity and cultural activity, it did have one less fortunate result. Assuming that Athens had permanently removed the Persian menace, most Greeks became overconfident. Surely, they thought, after such an embarrassing defeat Darius would never again dare to attack Greece. But this was a dangerously short-sighted view. Indeed, in the early 480s, while Athens basked in glory, Darius was already planning a new and larger European invasion force. According to Herodotus:

> When the news of the battle of Marathon reached Darius . . . his anger against Athens, already great enough on account of the assault on Sardis, was even greater, and he was more than ever determined to make war on Greece. Without loss of time he dispatched couriers to the various states under his dominion with orders to raise an army much larger than before; and also warships, transports, horses, and grain. So the royal command went round; and all Asia was in an uproar for three years, with the best men being enrolled in the army for the invasion of Greece.

But Darius never lived to fulfill his vengeance against Athens. He died in 486 and his son Xerxes became Persia's new Great King. To commemorate his ascendancy, Xerxes ordered the following inscription carved on a monument in Persepolis: "A great god is Ahura-Mazda, who created this earth, who created man, who created peace for man; who made Xerxes the king, king of kings." Persia's new leader was eager to carry on many of his father's policies, including the invasion of Greece. But in 484, a rebellion erupted in Egypt, demanding Xerxes' attention and forcing him to put off the European expedition. Another revolt in

*A relief depicts Xerxes, who became Persia's king after the death of his father, Darius. Xerxes, too, wanted to avenge the defeat at Marathon.*

Total Victory: The Greeks Make Europe Possible **71**

483, this one in the former Babylonia, created further delays. It was not until 482 that the Great King resumed preparations for a full-scale invasion of the Greek mainland.

## Athens's "Wooden Wall"

By this time, the Greeks, who had been receiving reports of these war preparations, finally began to appreciate the seriousness of the situation. Worried about the new Persian threat, Athenian leaders turned, as Greeks often did, to the Delphic oracle for guidance in making policy. The oracle warned of possible disaster for the city, declaring that only a "wooden wall" would save Athens from destruction. Realizing that the oracle's statements were usually cryptic, or laced with hidden meanings, the Athenians hotly debated the identity of the wooden wall. Aris-

*Pythia, one of Delphi's famed oracles. The Greeks consulted the oracle about their fate in a future battle with the Persians.*

*Themistocles, depicted beardless in this later Roman cameo, interpreted the Greek oracle's words to mean that the Athenians needed to build a navy.*

tides, often called "the Just" because of his honesty and fairness, argued that the oracle referred to a huge wooden stockade enclosing the Acropolis. If the Athenians built such a structure, he said, it would keep the Persians out.

Themistocles had a different interpretation. Maintaining his support of sea power, he insisted that the oracle's reference to a wooden wall described a large fleet of ships. At the time, the Athenians, still considering their polis to be primarily a land power, had only about seventy ships. Themistocles seems to have been the only city leader at the time who clearly foresaw that control of the sea was the key to Athens's future. According to the fifth-century B.C. Greek historian Thucydides:

> Themistocles was a man who most clearly presents the phenomenon of natural genius. . . . He showed both the best grasp of an emergency situation at the shortest notice, and the most far-reaching appreciation of probable further developments. . . . No man so well foresaw the advantages and disadvantages of a course in the still uncertain future. In short . . . he was the best of all men at determining promptly what had to be done.

And what Athens had to do, said Themistocles, was to build two hundred new, modern warships before it was too late.

But building ships and training crews, especially so many of each, was an expensive proposition. Even Themistocles was not sure where to find the money. It was at this crucial moment, early in the year 482 B.C., that both he and the city were able to

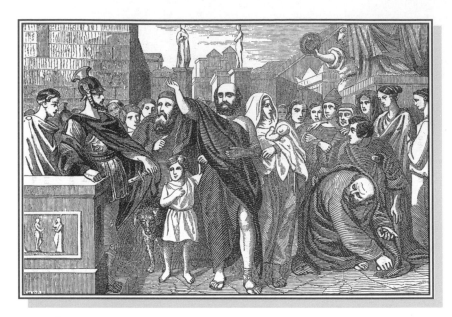

*Aristides is banished from Athens in 482 B.C.*

take advantage of an unexpected and timely stroke of luck. As Michael Grant explains:

> At this time rich new veins of silver ore were found on Attic territory, at Laurium, where the mines of that metal were [already] Athens' largest industrial asset. As was customary in Greek city-states—to which . . . economic planning was alien—a proposal was made that this surplus revenue should be distributed among the citizen body.

The new veins' initial silver yield alone was estimated to be worth 100 talents, or about 600,000 drachmas, at a time when 1 drachma could support a middle-class family for a day. Since Athens then had about 50,000 voting citizens, each would receive 12 drachmas. But in impassioned speeches to the Assembly, Themistocles argued that distributing the money this way would be foolish in view of the very real Persian threat. He managed to persuade the government to allot the funds to naval development, instead. Furious, Aristides continued to advocate beefing up the army and land defenses, and his political opponents helped engineer his ostracism and banishment late in 482.

## Seven Days and Seven Nights

Themistocles' 200 warships, completed in 480 after a crash building program, came just in time. Overseeing his final war preparations, Xerxes spent the winter of 481 in Sardis. In the spring he launched the greatest invasion force the world had ever seen. Modern historians estimate that his land forces numbered about

200,000 soldiers. Added to this were supply and support personnel and also sailors, for a fleet of 800 to 1,000 ships—probably another 250,000 to 300,000 men. In order for this vast group to cross the Hellespont, Xerxes' engineers built two bridges consisting of wooden platforms spanning the decks of rows of ships anchored close together.

During the weeks that the bridges were under construction, Xerxes clearly revealed his arrogant, mean-spirited, and childish nature. First, his chief official at Sardis asked that the oldest of his five sons be excused from military service, fearing that if all five died in the campaign, the family line would be wiped out. The Great King responded to this reasonable request by having the son cut in half, the pieces mounted on posts, and marching his army between them.

Soon afterward, a sudden windstorm wrecked the nearly completed boat-bridges. Enraged, Xerxes ordered the engineers beheaded. He then had several soldiers with whips lash the Hellespont waters in a bizarre attempt to punish the sea. When new bridges were completed, the whippers stood by and lashed at the soldiers and horses as they marched across the strait. The one group that probably escaped the lash was the king's personal bodyguard, an elite and supposedly invincible unit of ten thousand crack troops known as "the Immortals." The crossing must have been an awesome sight, as Herodotus's description hints:

> The first to cross were the Ten Thousand [Immortals], all with wreaths on their heads, and these were followed by the mass of troops of all the nations [under Persian rule]. Their crossing occupied the whole of the first day. On the next day the first over were the thousand horsemen, and the contingent which marched with spears reversed—these, too, all wearing

*The bridge of boats Xerxes and his vast army used to cross the Hellespont.*

According to Herodotus, when the Persian army approached the pass of Thermopylae, Xerxes sent a scout on horseback to observe the Greek position and learned something about the unique character of the Spartan hoplites:

The Persian rider approached the camp and took a thorough survey of all he could see—which was not, however, the whole Greek army; for the men on the further side of the wall . . . were out of sight. He did, none the less, carefully observe the troops who were stationed on the outside of the wall. At that moment these happened to be the Spartans, and some of them were stripped for exercise, while others were combing their hair. The Persian spy watched them in astonishment; nevertheless he made sure of their numbers, and of everything else he needed to know, as accurately as he could, and then quietly rode off. No one attempted to catch him, or took the least notice of him. Back in his own camp he told Xerxes what he had seen. Xerxes was bewildered; the truth, namely that the Spartans were preparing to . . . deal [with] death with all their strength, was beyond his comprehension, and what they were doing seemed to him merely absurd.

wreaths. Then came the sacred horses and the sacred chariot, and after them Xerxes himself with his spearmen and his [personal] thousand horsemen. The remainder of the army brought up the rear. . . . From the European shore Xerxes watched his troops coming over under the whips. The crossing occupied seven days and nights without a break.

Xerxes was confident his might would strike terror into the Greeks, and once his whole army was in Thrace he sent messengers with the customary demands for earth and water to most of the poleis. A few mainly northern states, located directly in the Persian army's path, submitted, but most others did not. The Athenian response was particularly bold. According to Plutarch:

When the king of Persia sent messengers into Greece, with an interpreter, to demand earth and water as an acknowledgement of subjection, Themistocles, by the consent of the people, seized upon the interpreter, and put him to death, for presuming to publish the barbarian orders in the Greek language; this is one of the actions he is commended for.

## The Greek Strategy

In anticipation of a Persian attack, representatives from thirty-one poleis met in Corinth, in the northern Peloponnesus about sixty miles southwest of Athens. Sparta and Athens dominated this so-called Congress of Corinth, deciding most of the overall strategy for Greece's defense. This was hardly surprising, since they were by far the two most powerful poleis. Sparta demanded and was granted command of both land and naval forces, to which Themistocles raised little or no objection. He shrewdly realized that his control of Athens's fleet, the largest single naval contingent in the united Greek armada, would give him the biggest say in naval strategy.

The Greek leaders knew that they would need a huge land force to oppose Xerxes' army and that assembling such a force from many small and scattered poleis would be difficult and time-consuming. It seemed wiser to follow Themistocles' advice and attempt to destroy the Persian fleet. Without ships to supply and support it, the Great King's huge army could not sustain itself for long. So the initial plan was for delaying tactics to keep the Persians out of southern Greece as long as possible while Themistocles and the other admirals prepared the fleet. The decision was made to send a small force to fortify the pass of Thermopylae, in the mountains about one hundred miles northwest of Athens. This was the only pass leading into southern Greece that was close enough to the sea to allow the Persians easy

access to their ships. Thermopylae also had the strategic advantage of being very narrow. As Herodotus put it:

> At one point the mountain and sea came so close together that the ground along the shore was only fifty feet wide. . . . This was the place at which the Greeks . . . thought they could resist the Persians successfully; for in this small space the enormous size of the Persian army would be of no advantage.

In July 480, Leonidas, who had succeeded Cleomenes as king of Sparta, took charge of the Thermopylae operation. At the time, Sparta was in the midst of another religious festival, which meant that the army was forbidden to march. So Leonidas called upon his personal bodyguard—three hundred elite troops who were bound by no laws but his. He made sure to take only men with living sons, so that no Spartan family line would be extinguished. The small band headed north, and along the way small contingents of troops from several poleis, including Tegea, Mantinaea, Corinth, Thespiae, Thebes, and Phocis, joined them. When the army reached Thermopylae a few days later, it numbered about seven thousand hoplites.

Soon, the gigantic Persian army approached and set up camp on the far side of the pass. A Persian scout told Xerxes how only

*To devise a plan to repel the Persian forces, Greek leaders met at Corinth (pictured). The Congress of Corinth was dominated by Athens and Sparta, Greece's leading poleis.*

a few Greeks held the pass, so the Great King assumed moving through would be a quick and simple operation. But Demaratus, the exiled Spartan king who was still advising Xerxes, warned that tangling with the Spartans could be dangerous. "These men," said Demaratus,

> have come to fight us for possession of the pass, and for that struggle they are preparing. . . . I assure you that if you can defeat these men and the rest of the Spartans who are still at home, there is no other people in the world who will dare to stand firm or lift a hand against you. You have now to deal with the finest kingdom of Greece, and with the bravest men.

## No Retreat

*Leonidas leads his few men against the Persians at Thermopylae. By greatly underestimating the Spartans, Xerxes lost many men to the Greek general.*

But Xerxes, thinking it ridiculous that so few men, no matter how brave, could stand up to his huge army, ignored Demaratus's advice. For days, the king ordered one attack after another, angrily and thoughtlessly sending waves of men into the pass. And each time, the Greeks repelled the assaults, butchering large numbers of Persians in the process. Even the Immortals could make no headway against the well-entrenched Greek position.

*A Greek traitor was responsible for Leonidas's defeat at Thermopylae, as Xerxes' troops were able to surround the soldiers and slaughter them.*

Just as it began to look as though Leonidas might be able to hold the pass indefinitely, a Greek civilian who lived in the area accepted gold in exchange for showing the Persians a little-known goat path through the hills. When Leonidas learned that a Persian force was rapidly closing in behind him, he realized his position was now hopeless. Dismissing most of the united troops, so as to spare them for later fighting, he and his three hundred Spartans remained at their posts. They had promised their countrymen and the other Greeks that they would defend the pass and, for Spartans, retreat was not an option. At the last moment, about one thousand other troops, including all seven hundred Thespians, refused to leave, bravely choosing to stand firm with Leonidas.

Eventually, the Persian trap closed around the tiny band of Greeks. Again, Xerxes ordered waves of men to attack, and the fighting became more frenzied and savage than ever. Leonidas fell, and when the Persians attempted to capture his body, the Spartans beat them back, inflicting heavy losses on Xerxes' men. Finally, the remaining Spartans and Thespians took a position on a small hill near the entrance of the pass, and, recalled Herodotus:

> Here they resisted to the last, with their swords, if they [still] had them, and, if not, with their hands and teeth, until the Persians, coming on them, from the front . . . and closing in from behind, finally overwhelmed them with missile weapons [arrows].

The deeds of the hoplites at Thermopylae, like those at Marathon, would never be forgotten. Capturing the single-minded courage of the fallen heroes was a stone marker later placed in the pass, bearing the simple message: "Tell them in Sparta, passerby, that carrying out their orders, here we lie."

## Where Will You Be Without Athens?

For Xerxes, the episode at Thermopylae, though technically a victory, had been humiliating and costly. Perhaps, as his men counted the Persian bodies, the Great King wished he had listened to Demaratus. Finding that a mere handful of men had killed almost twenty thousand of his own, the enraged king ordered Leonidas's head cut off and mounted on a pole for his troops to view as they filed through the pass.

Xerxes now marched south unopposed. On or about September 17, 480 B.C., he entered Athens, finding to his surprise that the city was largely deserted. Themistocles had wisely used his new ships to evacuate the populace to Salamis and other nearby islands. The only remaining people were a few die-hards who had barricaded themselves on the summit of the Acropolis. After storming their hideout and slaying them, Xerxes burned much of the city, including the half-finished Parthenon. The Great King felt that he had at last achieved his father's revenge for the burning of Sardis some eighteen years before.

Meanwhile, the Greek admirals readied their fleet for battle. All but Themistocles wanted to abandon Attica and take up a defensive position at the Isthmus of Corinth, many miles to the south. But he vehemently insisted that the Greeks make their stand at Salamis. According to Herodotus, Themistocles declared:

> It is now in your power to save Greece if you take my advice and engage the enemy's fleet here at Salamis, instead of withdrawing to the Isthmus. . . . If you fight there, it will have to be in the open sea, and that will be greatly to our disadvantage, with our smaller numbers. . . . [Whereas, at Salamis] we shall be fighting in narrow waters, and there, with our inferior numbers, we shall win. . . . Fighting in a confined space favors us but the open sea favors the enemy.

*Xerxes (left) and Themistocles, whose forces opposed each other in a naval battle at Salamis.*

When he encountered continued opposition to his plan, Themistocles angrily informed the other admirals that he was not giving them a choice. If they did not do as he said, he would immediately load all of the Athenians onto his ships and sail away to the western Mediterranean, there to establish a new city of Athens. "Where will you be without the Athenian fleet?" he thundered. Realizing that without Athens's navy, defeat was certain, the admirals relented and the Greek fleet converged on the narrow strait separating Salamis from southern Attica.

## Blood in the Waters

On September 20, Xerxes ordered his warships, perhaps 500 to 600 in number, into the strait. Unlike Themistocles and the other Greek admirals, who stood on the ships alongside their men, the Great King sat well out of harm's way on a throne hastily erected on a hill overlooking the waterway. Seeing that the Greeks had fewer than 340 vessels, he once again assumed that their inferior numbers would assure him an easy victory.

But Xerxes was in for still another surprise. Almost at once, the Greeks attacked and hemmed in the masses of Persian vessels on one side of the strait. Just as Themistocles had predicted, the Persians' greater numbers proved to be a disadvantage. "Most of the Persian vessels were lost," Herodotus recalled, "when their ships in the front rank were beaten, and turned to flee, for the commanders in the ships to the rear continued to press forward. . . . So the ships coming forward and ships retreating got in each other's way." As Xerxes watched in horror, the Greek hoplites and sailors slaughtered his men by the thousands. The playwright Aeschylus, who fought here as well as at Marathon, later recalled the massacre in his play *The Persians:*

> Then, the torrent of [the] Persian fleet bore up; but when the press of shipping jammed there in the strait, then none could help another, but [the] ships fouled [entangled] each other with their rams, and sheared away each other's banks of oars. But the Greek ships, skillfully handled . . . struck in[ward]; till hulls rolled over, and the sea itself was hidden, strewn with their wreckage, dyed with [the] blood of men. The [Persian] dead lay thick on all the reefs and beaches.

That day, more than two hundred Persian ships went to the bottom of the strait and many others were captured or damaged. The Greeks lost only forty ships. This crushing defeat, engineered by Themistocles, completely changed the face of the Persian campaign. As historian A. R. Burn remarks, "For the first time in Xerxes's war, Greek soldiers had taken the offensive and destroyed a Persian unit, and within sight of the king. Truly, the tide had turned."

## Honest Aristides

Aristides "the Just" fought at Marathon as one of Athens's ten elected generals, where he distinguished himself by fighting valiantly in the dangerous, thinned center of the phalanx. He also led the Athenian hoplites at the battle of Plataea. Perhaps the most famous story about Aristides, however, does not concern his battlefield exploits. According to Plutarch and other ancient sources, during the vote to ostracize and banish him in 482 B.C., he proved his extraordinary honesty and fairness at great cost to himself. Supposedly, a man who did not recognize him approached him. The man explained that he did not know how to write and asked Aristides to write a name for him on his pottery shard, or ostrakon. "Whose name shall I write?" asked Aristides. "Please write 'Aristides,'" the man replied. The surprised Aristides inquired, "But why? Has Aristides harmed you in some way?" "Oh, no," said the man. "In fact I would not know him if I saw him. I'm just sick and tired of hearing everyone call him 'the Just'!" After a moment's thought, Aristides silently wrote his own name on the shard, handed it to the man, and went on his way.

Humiliated and frustrated, Xerxes took several thousand troops and departed for Asia Minor. But he left Mardonius behind in Greece with a substantial land force of 150,000 soldiers. The Great King's orders were, no doubt, to destroy the puny Greek armies and subdue and burn as many cities as possible. It must have come as a shock to Mardonius when, after wintering in central Greece, he found himself facing a far from puny united Greek army. In the summer of 479, hoplites from all over the mainland converged on the Persians near Plataea. Among them were 20,000 Peloponnesians, including 5,000 from Sparta, the largest force ever fielded by that polis. Aristides the Just, whom Themistocles had generously recalled from exile, led 8,000 Athenians. In all, the Greeks numbered about 100,000, by far the biggest united Greek army up to that time. In a massive and hard-fought pitched battle, the Greeks, led by Spartan general Pausanias, nearly wiped out the Persian army.

*In the battle at Salamis the Greeks quickly beat the Persians, whose numerical advantage proved to be their downfall in the narrow strait.*

*The Spartans face the Persians in the battle of Plataea, which again favored the Greeks. After this battle, Xerxes gave up trying to conquer the Greeks.*

On the same day as the battle of Plataea, or perhaps a few days later, the Greeks struck the Persians at Mycale on the coast of Asia Minor. A force led by Spartan king Leotychidas landed on the coast, raced inland, and assaulted the Persians' camp, sending them into a wild retreat. The heartened Ionians took advantage of the opportunity and turned on their masters. Within days, Ionia was free once again. Fortunately for Xerxes, he had already returned to Susa by the time the Greeks attacked. Thereafter, he gave up the idea of conquering Greece, and no other Persian army ever entered Europe again.

## The Spirit of Human Freedom

The total victory of Greece over Persia, of West over East, had taken more than eleven years. It had begun with the heroic charge of the hoplites on the field of Marathon, an unexpected event that had halted Persia's certain expansion into Europe. The later battles against Xerxes' hordes had served to confirm a fact established at Marathon—namely that the Greek hoplite was the most effective soldier in the world. This meant that, at least for the moment, the Greeks no longer needed to fear attack from any quarter. Freedom for all Greeks, including the long-suffering Ionians, was assured.

The victory also filled the Greeks with another kind of confidence—pride in an immense accomplishment. They had demonstrated to the world—and also to themselves—that they, like their ancestors at Troy, were capable of glorious deeds. And the defeat of the greatest empire in the world seemed only the first

# The Majestic Parthenon

During Athens's "Golden Age" in the sixty years following Greece's victory over Persia, the city underwent a virtual cultural explosion and produced some of the greatest artistic and literary works in world history. The work that became an eternal symbol of Athens's glory, and of classical Greece in general, was the Parthenon, the temple dedicated to the city's patron goddess, Athena. Erected at the summit of the Acropolis, this magnificent structure could be seen for miles in every direction. Built between 447 and 438 B.C. by the architect Ictinus and the sculptor Phidias, the Parthenon was 237 feet long, 110 feet wide, 60 feet high, and contained about 22,000 tons of marble. Inside, in a large front room called the *cella*, stood Phidias's awesome statue of the goddess. This figure, over 40 feet high, depicted Athena holding a smaller figure of Nike, goddess of victory, in one hand and a hoplite's spear and shield in the other. The statue was made of wood, ivory, and over 2,500 pounds of pure gold. Behind the *cella* was a smaller "treasury" room, where jewelry, vases, and other offerings to the goddess were stored. The outside of the building was decorated with statues and sculpted scenes depicting stories from mythology and painted with bright colors, especially reds and blues. Though today the Parthenon is a crumbling, roofless ruin, even this mere shell of its former glory retains a noble and majestic quality, testifying to the brilliance and vision of its builders.

*The interior of the Parthenon featured a huge, 40-foot-high statue of Athena. The Parthenon was built to honor Athena, who, many Greeks believed, had helped them defeat the Persians.*

step toward other, equally noteworthy achievements. In this way, wrote historian W.G. Hardy, the victory over Persia became "the torch to set fire to the brilliance of the great age of the Greeks. There was a tremendous upswelling of confidence . . . [and now] the Greeks felt there was nothing they could not attempt."

This was especially true of the Athenians. In the decades following Persia's defeat, Athens experienced a cultural outburst the like of which the world had never seen before and would never see again. Atop the Acropolis, replacing Athena's temple (destroyed by the Persians), rose a new Parthenon, a building unequalled in majesty and beauty throughout the ages. From ancient Rome to modern Washington, D.C., countless public buildings have carried the unmistakable imprint of Greek temple architecture. Athenian drama and philosophy, from the grand tragedies of Aeschylus and Sophocles, to the shrewd insights of Socrates and Plato, became the intellectual cornerstones of Western literature and are still routinely studied today. Athenian work in painting, sculpture, and scientific inquiry was equally stunning. In general, Athens and other Greek states left behind an artistic and literary legacy that has inspired the world ever since.

Perhaps even more important, the Greek victory marked one of the decisive events of world history because it kept an Eastern power from conquering Europe. In fact, the Greek defeat of Persia,

*Greek citizens welcome the victors at Salamis with a great celebration. The victory over the Persians would lead the Greeks, especially the Athenians, to greater cultural and artistic heights.*

*An ancient Greek temple is a testament to the way in which Greek culture spread worldwide. Many modern buildings are built to resemble those of the ancient Greeks.*

historian Will Durant comments, "made Europe possible. It won for Western civilization the opportunity to develop its own economic life . . . its own political institutions." In the two centuries following the Greek Golden Age, Greek culture spread across much of the known world. It inspired the Romans, who at the time were building a mighty empire in the central Mediterranean. When Rome's civilization eventually eclipsed that of Greece, the Romans perpetuated Greek artistic, architectural, and literary styles, producing what later scholars dubbed the Greco-Roman "classical" style.

Rome itself eventually declined and gave way to many tiny European kingdoms. And these realms subsequently grew into the nations of Europe, which, in time, explored and colonized nearly every corner of the globe. This means that modern European-based nations such as the United States and Canada can trace their growth straight back, through an unbroken chain of Western historical events, to the Greeks who fought at Marathon, Salamis, and Plataea. There can be little doubt, then, that had Datis and Artaphernes managed to defeat the hoplites at Marathon, giving Persia a foothold in Europe, the history of the world would have been profoundly different.

Thus, in a sense, Western civilization, with all of its many good qualities, as well as its many faults, is a product of what the Greeks felt, thought, and did long ago. Among the qualities the Greeks imparted to later generations of Westerners, none was or still is more cherished than the spirit of human freedom. And perhaps nowhere else has that spirit been expressed in more simple and straightforward fashion than in the words carved on the ancient monument on the battlefield at Plataea:

> The Greeks, when, by their courage and their might,
>   They had repelled the Persian in the fight,
> Banding together for Greece's future liberty,
>   Erected this [monument] to Zeus, who guards the free.

# For Further Reading

Isaac Asimov, *The Greeks: A Great Adventure.* Boston: Houghton Mifflin, 1965. An excellent, entertaining overview of the ancient Greeks, with an emphasis on their importance to later cultures.

David Bellingham, *An Introduction to Greek Mythology.* Secaucus, NJ: Chartwell Books, 1989. Explains the major Greek myths and legends and their importance to the ancient Greeks. Contains many beautiful photos and drawings.

Peter Connolly, *The Greek Armies.* Morristown, NJ: Silver Burdett, 1979 A fine, detailed study of Greek armor, weapons, and battle tactics and how they evolved over the centuries in ancient Greece. Filled with colorful, appropriate illustrations. Highly recommended.

Homer, *Iliad.* Retold by Barbara Leonie Picard. New York: Oxford University Press, 1960. A simple, entertaining version of the classic tale of the Trojan War, translated and presented specifically for young readers.

Don Nardo, *Ancient Greece.* San Diego: Lucent Books, 1994. A detailed overview of ancient Greek history, providing a context for understanding the Greek and Persian Wars and their significance to the development of Western civilization.

Susan Peach and Anne Millard, *The Greeks.* London: Usborne, 1990 A general overview of the history, culture, and myths of ancient Greece. Filled with excellent color illustrations.

Michael Wood, *In Search of the Trojan War.* New York: New American Library, 1985. A fascinating and well-researched account of the various archaeologists and expeditions that have worked at Troy. Tells how archaeologist Heinrich Schliemann and others proved that the events of Homer's *Iliad* were true and includes some excellent reconstructions showing what the city might have looked like in its prime.

# Works Consulted

Alessandro Bausani, *The Persians: From the Earliest Days to the Twentieth Century*. London: Elek Books, 1971. A thorough, readable overview of Persian civilization by one of the foremost scholars on the subject.

C. M. Bowra, *The Greek Experience*. New York: New American Library, 1957. An excellent general discussion of ancient Greek history and culture by a fine historian and writer.

James Henry Breasted, *Ancient Times: A History of the Early World*. New York: Ginn, 1944. Somewhat dated but still masterful and concisely written account of ancient history.

A. R. Burn, *Persia and the Greeks· The Defense of the West, 546–478 B.C.* London: Edward Arnold, 1962. A massive, well-researched account of the Greek and Persian Wars, with an emphasis on their importance to later European culture.

Walter Donlan and James Thompson, "The Charge at Marathon," *Classical Journal*, vol. 71, 1976, and "The Charge at Marathon Again," *Classical World*, vol. 72, 1979. Examinations of whether the famous charge described by Herodotus as being performed "at the run" could actually have occurred as reported, since it is doubtful that men wearing more than forty pounds of armor could have run a mile and still have had enough energy left to fight a grueling battle.

Will Durant, *The Life of Greece*. New York: Simon and Schuster, 1966. A detailed, scholarly study of all aspects of Greek civilization, with special emphasis placed on the various aspects of everyday life, attitudes, and beliefs. Victor Ehrenberg, *From Solon to Socrates: Greek History and Civilization During the Sixth and Fifth Centuries B.C.* London: Methuen, 1968. An insightful, scholarly study of the period, including the events of the Greek and Persian Wars.

J. A. S. Evans, "Herodotus and the Battle of Marathon," *Historia*, vol. 4213, 1993. A fascinating discussion of the famous battle as reported by the ancient historian.

Michael Grant, *The Classical Greeks*. New York: Scribner's, 1989. A collection of short but highly informative biographies of some of the most important figures in Greek history, including several leading figures in the Greek and Persian Wars.

Michael Grant, *The Founders of the Western World: A History of Greece and Rome*. New York: Scribner's, 1991. A fine general overview of ancient Greek civilization.

Michael Grant, *The Rise of the Greeks*. New York: Macmillan, 1987. A detailed, scholarly study of early Greek civilization, including the formation of city-states and Greek attitudes and beliefs.

Victor Davis Hanson, *The Western Way to War: Infantry Battle in Classical Greece*. New York: Oxford University Press, 1989. A masterful, very readable study of all aspects of ancient Greek hoplite warfare. Professor Hanson builds his study around the premise that "the Greeks' stark way of battle left us with what is now a burdensome legacy in the West: a presumption that battle under any guise other than no-nonsense, head-to-head confrontation between sober enemies is or should be unpalatable."

Victor Davis Hanson, ed. *Hoplites: The Classical Greek Battle Experience*. New York: Routledge, 1993. An excellent collection of scholarly articles concerning ancient hoplite warfare, including: "Hoplite Technology in Phalanx Battle," "The Killing Zone," and "Hoplites and the Gods: The Dedication of Captured Arms and Armor."

Herodotus, *Histories*. Translated by Aubrey de Selincourt. New York: Penguin Books, 1972. An excellent translation of the ancient Greek historian's detailed account of the Greek and Persian Wars, the most important primary source material for these events, including the battle of Marathon.

A. J. Holladay, "Hoplites and Heresies," *Journal of Hellenic Studies*, vol. 102, 1982. An examination and criticism of several new views of hoplite warfare.

John Lazenby, *The Defense of Greece*. Bloomington, IL: David Brown, 1993. A comprehensive modern examination of the Greek and Persian Wars.

Peter Levi, *Atlas of the Greek World*. New York; Facts On File, 1984. A handsome edition that provides an overview of Greek civilization, with many maps, color photos, drawings, and interesting sidebars about Greek art and customs.

W. McLeod, "The Bowshot at Marathon," *Journal of Hellenic Studies*, vol. 90, 1970. An examination of the range of the arrows fired by the Persians at Marathon and how it may have affected the strategy of the Greek charge.

Plutarch, *Themistocles* and *Aristides*, in *Lives of the Noble Grecians and Romans*. Chicago: Encyclopedia Britannica, 1952. These short biographies by the ancient Greek/Roman writer are valuable assets in reconstructing the military and political events of fifth-century B.C. Athens. Both Themistocles and Aristides fought at Marathon and Plutarch's mention of the battle helps to supplement Herodotus's account.

A. M. Snodgrass, *Arms and Armour of the Greeks*. Ithaca, NY: Cornell University Press, 1967. A very detailed, scholarly study of ancient Greek armor and weapons, supported by evidence from ancient vase paintings, literature, and other sources.

Percy Sykes, *A History of Persia*. London: Macmillan, 1958. A large (two-volume) and masterful study of Persian civilization. Recommended mainly for scholars and serious students of the subject.

# Index

Acropolis, 16
  burning of, 80
  Parthenon at, 70, 84, 85
Aeschylus, 63, 81, 85
architecture, 18, 84, 85, 86
archons, 17-18
Aristagoras
  attack on Sardis, 44
  seeking of Greek aid, 42-43
  united Ionians, 42
Aristides
  at Marathon battle, 56, 57,
    63, 81
  at Plataea battle, 81, 82
  on meaning of oracle's
    warning, 72-73
  ostracism of, 74, 81
armies. *See* hoplites; Persian
  Empire
*Arms and Armor of the Greeks*
  (Snodgrass), 39
Artaphernes, 50, 52, 86
  decision to abandon Athens
    invasion, 65
  strategy at Marathon, 56
Asia Minor
  Cyaxares' invasion of, 20-21
  Cyrus the Great's invasion
    of, 26, 27-28
  territorial disputes over, 13
  *see also* Ionia
Assyria, 19, 20
Athena, 68, 70, 84
Athens
  Black Sea grain route, 34
  building of sea power, 47-48,
    73-74
  celebrations held in, 68, 69
  commercial successes, 69-70
  cultural achievements, 69-70,
    84, 85, 86
  defiance of Darius I, 50
  hoplites from, 10, 52, 54, 55
    at Plataea battle, 82
    command of, 56
    feted after Marathon, 69

leading polis
  after Marathon battle, 69-70
  reasons for, 17
oracle's warning to, 72-73
Persian wrath toward
  invasion efforts, 50-51, 71,
    76-77
    after Marathon, 50, 51-52,
      55, 65
    after Thermopylae, 80
  reasons for, 41, 44-45
political progress in
  archon's role, 17-18
  Cleisthenes', 35
  ostracism, 70, 74, 81
  Pisistratus's, 35
  written laws, 18
reaction to Persian invasion
  of Thrace, 33-34, 76
role as champion of liberty, 37
role in Ionian rebellion, 43, 44

Babylonia, 19, 72
  Cyrus's conquest of, 31
  hanging gardens of, 20
  taxes paid to Persians, 32
battles
  sound of, 66
  viewing of bodies after,
    66-68
  *see also specific battles*
Bausani, Alessandro
  on class differences, 24
  on rise of Persian Empire, 21
Bias, of Priene, 30-31
bireme, 46
Bury, A.R., 81

Callimachus, 56, 57, 63
Cambyses, 31, 35
Canada, 86
children, 36, 47
Chios, 45
city-states (poleis)
  commonalities between,
    17-18

  failed to help Athenians, 55
  failed to help Ionians, 31
  fear of Persians, 33, 38
  fighting between, 37
  growth of, 19
  origins of, 16
  population of, 17
Cleisthenes, 35
Cleomenes, 42-43, 50
Connolly, Peter, 36
Corinth, 77
  Congress of, 76, 77
  Isthmus of, 80
Crocsus, 28, 29
Cyaxares, 20
  effort to conquer Asia Minor,
    21
Cynegirus, 63
Cyrus II ("the Great"), 21, 22,
  24, 26
  attacks on Asia Minor, 27
  conquest of Ionia, 28, 29, 30
  desire to invade Europe, 28
  expansion of Persian
    borders, 31
  on threat from Greeks, 30
  strong leadership of, 28

Darius I, 31
  building projects, 31-32, 33
  decision to invade Greece,
    50-51
  desire for revenge, 44-45
  reaction to Battle of
    Marathon, 71
  reaction to Ionian rebellion,
    41
  self-description, 32-33
Datis, 50, 52, 86
  decision to abandon Athens
    invasion, 65
  strategy at Marathon, 56
death, 66, 67, 76
Delphi, 69
  oracle, 28-29, 72-73
Demaratus

# Picture Credits

Cover photo: The Bettmann Archive

Archive Photos, 26, 48 (left), 74, 80 (left), 86

The Bettmann Archive, 11, 12, 13, 16, 29 (both), 30, 34, 37, 42, 48 (right), 54, 57, 62, 65, 70 (top), 72, 77, 78, 79, 83

Library of Congress, 19 (left)

North Wind Picture Archives, 19 (right), 24, 36, 46, 49, 53, 59, 60, 64, 68, 69, 73, 75, 80 (right), 85

Stock Montage, Inc., 14, 18, 20, 21, 23, 25, 27, 31, 39, 51, 70 (bottom), 71, 82, 84

## About the Author

Don Nardo is an award-winning author whose more than sixty books cover a wide range of topics. His science, environmental, and medical titles include *Lasers, Gravity, Germs, Vaccines, Dinosaurs, Vitamins and Minerals, Ozone, Oil Spills,* and *Exercise.* Among his history and government studies are *Democracy, The U.S. Congress, The U.S. Presidency, The War of 1812, The Mexican-American War, Braving the New World,* and biographies of Thomas Jefferson, Franklin D. Roosevelt, and William Lloyd Garrison. Mr. Nardo's specialty is the ancient world, especially the classical civilizations of Greece and Rome. In addition to this volume on the Greek and Persian Wars, he has written the historical overviews *Ancient Greece, The Roman Republic, The Roman Empire, Greek and Roman Theater, The Punic Wars,* and biographies of Cleopatra and Julius Caesar. In addition, he has written screenplays and teleplays, including works for Warner Brothers and ABC-TV. Mr. Nardo lives with his wife, Christine, on Cape Cod, Massachusetts.